Talking with Confidence
for the
Painfully Shy

Talking

with

Confidence

for the

Painfully
Shy

■

Don Gabor

 THREE RIVERS PRESS • NEW YORK

Published by Three Rivers Press, New York, New York.
Member of the Crown Publishing Group.

Random House, Inc. New York, Toronto, London, Sydney, Auckland
www.randomhouse.com

THREE RIVERS PRESS is a registered trademark and the Three Rivers Press
colophon is a trademark of Random House, Inc.

Printed in the United States of America

Design by Debbie Glasserman

Library of Congress Cataloging-in-Publication Data
Gabor, Don.
Talking with confidence for the painfully shy / by Don Gabor.
Includes bibliographical references and index.
1. Conversation. 2. Bashfulness. I. Title.
BJ2121.G33   1997   153.6—dc21   96-49433

ISBN 0-517-88677-4

10   9   8

■ Dedication and Acknowledgments

My special thanks goes to my wife, Eileen Cowell, for her superb editing and support throughout this project. I want to thank my editor at Crown Publishers, Sharon Squibb, for her many excellent suggestions and guidance. I appreciate *Sprint*'s help in developing the concept of "telebonding." I owe my agent, Sheree Bykofsky, a debt of gratitude for her hard work and skill in negotiating this book contract. I also want to thank my family, my friends, and office cat Sophie for their continued enthusiasm and inspiration. Finally, I dedicate this book to every shy person motivated to improve his or her ability to communicate.

■ Contents

■ Introduction

Shyness—the bane of your existence—rears its ugly head yet once again! Perhaps it is when a friend at work says, "We're having a party next weekend. Would you like to come?" Or maybe your stomach fills with knots when your boss chooses you to make a stand-up presentation at a meeting. Or a sudden case of "dry mouth" twists your tongue into a pretzel during a job interview and then you miss a golden networking opportunity.

If you consider yourself shy, you are not alone. Studies show that more than 75 percent of adults characterize themselves as "shy" in one or more social and business situations. In fact, many people are not just shy about public speaking, but are terrified to enter a roomful of strangers, meet new people, and start conversations.

How This Book Can Help You

Talking with Confidence for the Painfully Shy is a book about "speaking in public." It presents proven techniques that I have taught to thousands of shy people—professionals, students, singles, and couples—who have attended my conversation workshops since 1980. I know these communication skills work because I personally use them in *every* social and business conversation I encounter. Based on the hundreds of letters I have received from past students and readers, I know these "tried and true" skills can help even the most reluctant communicator become more open and talkative.

As you master the skills in this book, you will conquer the butterflies you feel in your stomach every time you meet and talk to others in social and business situations. This hands-on guide provides the communication tools for getting past your shyness and building the confidence you need to talk with poise and power. Each chapter shows you how to overcome nervousness, fear of rejection, and even potential hostility when talking in small and large groups. Easy-to-follow examples and exercises demonstrate dozens of surefire communication skills, tips, and techniques. The primary objective of this book is to help you conquer shyness and talk confidently in every social and business situation.

How to Use This Book

I have divided *Talking with Confidence for the Painfully Shy* into three parts: "Kicking the Shyness Habit," "Speaking in Social Situations," and "Speaking in Business Situations." You can start at the beginning and read all the way through to the end or choose a specific chapter that addresses your particular need. Part One, "Kicking the Shyness Habit," focuses on getting over what has probably been a lifelong problem—chronic shyness. In three short chapters you'll learn how to break the shyness habit by changing the way you talk to yourself, sharing your expertise and interests, and showing your sense of humor.

Part Two, "Speaking in Social Situations," focuses on informal social situations in which you can interact and express yourself more effectively. In six concise chapters you'll learn how to master small talk, mingle at parties, host a get-together, extricate yourself from uncomfortable conversations, present toasts, and even build relationships on the telephone.

Part Three, "Speaking in Business Situations," concentrates on communicating with clarity and assurance in more formal business environments. In these ten jam-packed chapters you'll learn how to interview for a new job, conduct a meeting, present a speech, softsell, negotiate, deal with difficult clients, facilitate a training session, talk business over meals, network at conventions, and even make business contacts on airplanes!

Getting Started

Some shy people have told me that they feel less inhibited in business situations than in social situations because in business everyone knows what to expect from one another. It's the small talk and mingling at parties that drives them to distraction. Others say that social situations are easier to cope with because of more relaxed rules of etiquette. Whether you are nervous and inhibited in social or business situations, remember that you can learn to relax and be more outgoing. If you are ready to change your life, then just turn the page and start learning how to break the shyness habit. It will surprise you how easily you can master these skills and get what you want out of life simply by *Talking with Confidence!*

part one

∎

Kicking
the
Shyness
Habit

1
■ Changing the Way You Talk to Yourself

"The tongue is the rudder of our ship."

—PROVERB

In this chapter you'll learn how to:

- **Break a pattern of shy behavior.**
- **Transform inhibiting "self-talk" into confidence-building statements.**
- **Practice constructive self-talk.**
- **Be more approachable.**

Mark Twain was considered one of America's wittiest writers and lecturers, but when it came to talking, even he didn't always know what to say. During a long-awaited meeting with General Ulysses S. Grant, Twain found himself at a loss for words. Grant, who was known for his unemotional demeanor, simply sat with an un-smiling face and waited for the country's most popular author to say something—funny or otherwise. As the silent seconds passed, Mark Twain's discomfort grew. Then inspiration struck and the comic genius said, "General, I seem to be a little embarrassed. Are you?"

Stop Reinforcing Your Shy Behavior

Everyone has embarrassing moments at one time or another. Think of how you feel when you meet a new person in a social or business situation. Do you get uncomfortable, tongue-tied, and nervous? Do your palms sweat and do you blush, giggle, or say ridiculous things? Is it pure agony to make small talk and carry on a conversation? Are you afraid of sounding foolish or offending the other person? Do you want to escape from the situation as quickly as possible? If responses such as these occur on a regular basis when you meet people, then you probably describe yourself as "shy."

Although you have been reserved for most of your life, there is a way to kick the shyness habit. You may not realize it, but how you talk to yourself plays a significant role in your level of shyness. When that little voice inside your head starts planting those old seeds of doubt, your nervous reactions are not far behind. This deflating "self-talk" depletes your confidence and reinforces shy behavior.

Replace Inhibiting "Self-Talk" with Confidence-Building Statements

The first step in breaking your pattern of shy behavior is to change how you talk to yourself. By replacing shy and often detrimental self-talk with confidence-building statements, you can initiate the process of changing how you feel. Whenever you hear that destructive voice in your head start to undermine your confidence, say to yourself, "Stop!" Then decide to replace subverting self-talk with constructive statements that build your self-esteem. The following chart shows typical shy self-talk and the words you can say instead to elevate your confidence.

STOP saying to yourself:	START saying to yourself:
"I never know what to say."	*"I'll show interest in others."*
"I hate meeting new people."	*"I want to make some new friends."*
"I can't do it."	*"I'll try it and see what happens."*
"I don't want to go to the party."	*"I might meet someone interesting."*
"I probably won't have any fun."	*"I can be amusing when I want to."*

"I'm boring."
"No one will want to talk to me."
"I wish I were better looking."
"This is an absolute waste of time."
"I always say the dumbest things."

"I'll discuss some of my interests."
"I'll be the first to say hello."
"I may not be ideal, but who is?"
"What do I have to lose?"
"It's how I say it that counts."

Three Steps to Rehearse Constructive Self-Talk

You can do three things to make constructive self-talk easier.

Step 1: Find a Quiet Time and Location Where Others Won't Interrupt You

First, establish a daily routine in which you can practice how you talk to yourself. Find a few quiet times and places during the day where you can spend a few tranquil minutes alone. Good times to rehearse are before breakfast, while you exercise, on breaks, after work, on walks, while you relax in the evening, or just before you go to sleep. The more you practice constructive self-talk, the faster you can change your shy behavior.

Step 2: Visualize a Specific Situation

Second, consider an upcoming situation in which you probably will feel inhibited. For example, perhaps you always get tongue-tied at your department's weekly meeting. Now use your imagination to visualize the situation as clearly as possible. See your coworkers making small talk while they wait for your supervisor to start the meeting. Notice where people sit and imagine what they say to each other. See how the meeting progresses and imagine what everyone says and does. The secret to effective visualizations is to fill in as many minute details as possible, including the time, room temperature, what people are wearing, and even their facial expressions.

Step 3: Picture and Describe Your Constructive Actions, Attitudes, and Feelings in the Situation

Imagine yourself interacting in a more outgoing manner with your coworkers and supervisor under these circumstances. Meticulously describe your actions, attitudes, and feelings in constructive terms and in the present tense. If a negative thought creeps in, acknowledge it as a confidence-buster and swiftly substitute it with positive self-talk. While visualizing a staff meeting, you might say to yourself:

"I want to ask an important question during the meeting."

"I can help other people in my department be more efficient."

"These weekly meetings are much more interesting when I share my ideas."

"My confidence shows when I actively participate and help solve problems."

"I feel like part of our team when I cooperate and contribute during the meeting."

Changing the Way You Talk to Yourself Creates a More Positive Self-Image

In the past, your shy self-talk resulted in shy behavior, but now you are starting to learn how to use constructive self-talk to create a more confident and outgoing manner. To overcome your shyness, you can write a new self-talk script and then practice it before each situation in which you expect to feel uncomfortable. By describing the positive actions, attitudes, and feelings you want to experience *before* they occur, you will gain confidence and poise.

You might be surprised at how quickly you can shatter that old pattern of shyness and become a more outspoken individual. You'll know that your constructive self-talk is working when in social and business situations you sit tall, walk tall, and seem self-assured. You will feel your confidence grow as your conversation becomes more creative and spontaneous. It all starts with the way you talk to yourself. Constructive self-talk changes the way you feel about yourself and sets the stage for kicking the shyness habit.

FIFTEEN WAYS TO OVERCOME SHYNESS

1. Stop depending on others to communicate for you in social or business situations.
2. Expand your social life outside the family.
3. Visualize yourself as an active, interested, and interesting conversationalist.
4. Find and emulate good conversationalists.
5. Use relaxation techniques before you go into social and business situations.
6. Gain conversational momentum by always practicing your communication skills.
7. Identify your conversational successes and pat yourself on the back.
8. Create a socializing schedule for yourself and stick to it.
9. Avoid judging yourself too harshly if you make a mistake or say the wrong thing.
10. Identify how others respond to you and keep doing what gets positive results.
11. Validate others by acknowledging their achievements and self-worth.
12. Graciously accept compliments by saying, "Thanks for saying so. I appreciate hearing that."
13. Talk to people who make you feel good about yourself.
14. Focus more on the other person than on yourself.
15. Give others the benefit of the doubt and they will do the same for you.

2

■ Turning Your Shyness into an Asset

"Though modesties be a virtue, bashfulness is a vice."

—PROVERB

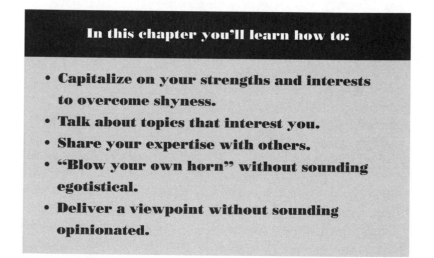

In this chapter you'll learn how to:

- **Capitalize on your strengths and interests to overcome shyness.**
- **Talk about topics that interest you.**
- **Share your expertise with others.**
- **"Blow your own horn" without sounding egotistical.**
- **Deliver a viewpoint without sounding opinionated.**

Although Benjamin Franklin was one of America's prominent inventors, diplomats, and public leaders, his abrupt manner with other people sometimes caused him unnecessary difficulties. According to one biography, Franklin came up with a unique self-improvement plan to correct the problem. He first listed his shortcomings, including being ill-tempered, impatient, and rude. Then he decided to focus on correcting them one at a time. Franklin's plan worked because he managed to overcome most of his bad habits within a year of the time that he made note of them.

Share Your Strengths, Interests, and Passions

You can use Benjamin Franklin's self-improvement plan—with a twist. List your strengths instead of your weaknesses and use them to become a more confident communicator. As a shy person, you may spend more time alone than you probably prefer, but it does give you opportunities to develop several interests and abilities. In the past you may have pursued these endeavors alone, but now you can break that pattern and share them with others.

The best way to begin is to ask yourself specific questions. What do you do well? What are you passionate about? Do you have a "green thumb"? Can you identify a valuable antique at a garage sale? Are you an American Civil War buff? Is music, art, or sports your passion? As you list your interests, always remember that what you do in life and your level of expertise in a chosen field is not as important as your willingness to share your enthusiasm and knowledge with the people you meet. On a sheet of paper, list some of your skills, passions, hobbies, and interests. Then write various ways you might use your abilities to help someone or expand your contacts with others. For example:

Now implement Ben Franklin's principle by tackling one issue at a time. Choose just *one* way you can share your avocations or expertise with a person or a group. For example, showing a new employee the "ropes" or joining a bowling league is an easy, low-risk way to chip away at your shyness. As you feel more confident, offer to conduct a team activity at work or volunteer to teach a course or workshop in your area of expertise at a local recreation center. When you demonstrate that you are willing to share your interests and strengths with others, people will admire and appreciate you. Your self-esteem will sky-rocket along with your confidence, and you'll naturally feel less shy and more talkative because you're involved in something that you feel enthusiastic about.

"Blow Your Own Horn" Without Sounding Egotistical

You may feel reluctant to tell others about your abilities out of fear of sounding like a show-off. Perhaps you are reluctant to reveal your accomplishments because you think that others might perceive you

I LIKE AND AM GOOD AT:

- Using a computer art program.
- Planning and completing long-term projects at work.
- Plumbing, electrical, and other home repairs.
- Playing volleyball and table tennis.
- Playing the guitar.
- Identifying valuable coins and stamps.
- Cooking an inexpensive gourmet meal.

I CAN SHARE THESE INTERESTS AND STRENGTHS WITH OTHERS BY:

- Helping a new person at work learn a computer program.
- Discussing with a coworker the possibility of working together on future projects.
- Teaching an adult-education course on easy home repairs.
- Organizing a local volleyball or table tennis tournament.
- Offering to teach a new friend a few guitar lessons.
- Inviting an interested acquaintance to attend a coin and stamp show.
- Asking a new friend to take a cooking class.

as conceited. Actually, if you blow your own horn gently, the opposite usually happens. Most people want to know something interesting and unique about you. This helps them understand what you are willing to talk about and if you have anything in common with them. Remember, many other people are just as shy as you, so letting them in on your passions, or "hot buttons," helps them feel more comfortable talking to you. For example, at a party when someone asks me what I like to do, I reply with something like:

"I'm a book person. I write books. I love to read books. I sell books. Books are my life!"

This answer usually evokes a question or two about the kinds of books I write and enjoy reading. After a few more thoughts about books and publishing, I make sure that the other person is also interested in this topic by inquiring, "What kinds of books do you enjoy reading?" or "Are you interested in writing and publishing, too?"

To let others know that you are willing to share your expertise, follow these examples:

"Oh, you want to learn how to play backgammon? I play with friends every weekend. If you want, I can show you the basic moves and strategies."

"If you'd like a few guitar lessons, just let me know. I used to play in a band."

"I heard you mention that you want to buy a used car, but you're afraid it might be a lemon. I'm pretty good when it comes to fixing cars. I'd be happy to look at the car for you and tell you what I think of its condition."

"I'm not a restaurant critic or anything like that, but I pride myself on knowing some great places to eat that don't cost an arm and a leg. If you'd like, I can give you some great restaurant recommendations for your upcoming visit."

A Few Words of Caution About Sharing Your Expertise
Avoid talking too much about a particular esoteric subject, offering too much unsolicited advice, discussing obscure concepts, using complicated terms and jargon, or exaggerating your abilities or achievements.

Playing the Expert Helps You Kick the Shyness Habit

When you talk about your passions and pursuits, your shyness takes a backseat. Those old butterflies may still crop up on occasion, but letting others in on your interests can do wonders to boost your confidence. New friends and old acquaintances will see you as a friendly person who enjoys sharing your expertise and enthusiasm with others.

EXPRESS YOUR VIEWS WITHOUT SOUNDING OPINIONATED

Do you sometimes get into disagreements while sharing your views? Or do you conceal your beliefs because you do not want to sound opinionated? Use the chart below to adjust your conversational style when expressing your opinions.

ENCOURAGES CONSTRUCTIVE EXCHANGE	SOUNDS CLOSED AND OPINIONATED
Discuss many sides of an issue before forming a conclusion.	Present a narrow viewpoint without seeing other possibilities.
Acknowledge another viewpoint even if it is different from yours.	Deny the validity of other viewpoints and feelings.
Accept that others may disagree.	Interrupt and do not listen.
Encourage others to express their opposing views.	Make personal attacks.
Support your views with facts.	Make emotional generalizations.
Find areas of agreement with others.	Argue over minor details and turn the conversation into a debate.

3
■ Using Humor to Overcome Shyness

"I wish I had a sense of humor, but I can never think of the right thing to say until everybody's gone home."

—CAROLE LOMBARD TALKING TO WILLIAM POWELL
IN THE MOVIE *MY MAN GODFREY*

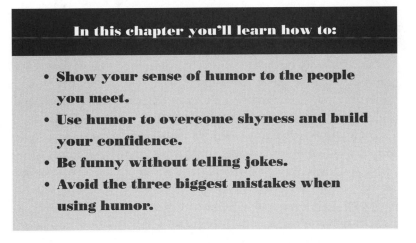

In this chapter you'll learn how to:

- **Show your sense of humor to the people you meet.**
- **Use humor to overcome shyness and build your confidence.**
- **Be funny without telling jokes.**
- **Avoid the three biggest mistakes when using humor.**

Comedian George Burns must have nearly swallowed his cigar when he found out that Ed Sullivan had revealed in his newspaper column that George wore a toupee. When Burns confronted him about mentioning this embarrassing personal information, Sullivan protested, "But George, I didn't think you'd mind." Burns responded with his sly smile and a puff of cigar smoke, "If I didn't mind, Ed, why would I wear a toupee?"

Humor Is Where You Find It

For a shy person, there's nothing funny about being uncomfortable in social situations, but using your sense of humor can help you become more outgoing and gregarious. Making a pun or a quip, or telling a short lighthearted story, adds zest to your conversations and encourages others to chime in with a joke of their own. Researchers have shown that humor really works to lower anxiety in social and business situations alike because laughter makes people more relaxed and receptive.

If you are like many shy people, you've got a good sense of humor, but you may be reluctant to show it. However, sharing a laugh with someone you've just met will make both of you feel more comfortable in the first few minutes of conversation. This easygoing attitude decreases your shyness and makes you appear more appealing and attractive.

Listen for the Humor Around You

You don't have to be the first one to crack a joke to show your sense of humor. There are many easy ways to share what tickles your funny bone. One way is to react to a clever or amusing remark. You need to be honest with your reactions, though, so don't fake a laugh if you don't think what you heard is funny. However, a sincere smile and laugh at a quip or amusing story sends a powerful signal of approval and makes the speaker feel good about talking to you. Listen carefully for droll remarks, dry wit, whimsical stories, puns, plays on words, or anything else that you can respond to with a chuckle or chortle. Your smile and laugh at someone's jest compliments him or her and shows you are listening.

You can also reveal that you appreciate someone else's sense of humor by stating the obvious—"You're funny!" or "You've got a great sense of humor." This friendly comment encourages that person to open up to you. When you respond to humor in a conversation, you send this message to the speaker:

> *"I like you and I enjoy your perspective. Thanks for sharing it with me."*

Reveal Your Sense of Humor
by Telling an Amusing Story

Can you remember some of the most amusing moments you've observed at a party, a wedding, or in another situation where something happened that made everyone laugh? For example, during my backyard wedding reception, my best man tossed a piece of wheat toast into the air as he wished my bride and me a happy life together. Unexpectedly, the airborne "toast" sailed into the hot tub. The guests howled!

Perhaps you have witnessed a "blooper" during an important event that left people laughing hysterically. To add humor to a conversation, tell funny real-life situations like these. Everyone has amusing stories to tell. The point is, you can share your sense of humor without being a stand-up comedian or clown. A few mildly amusing anecdotes, or *short* stories, that are real and easily related can get people laughing. The closer the story relates to the topic of conversation, the funnier it will be. For example, if you are at a fund-raising event, you could tell a variation of this story:

> *"Being at this charity event reminds me of a story I once heard about the comedian Jack Benny. You know, of course, that while his Hollywood image was that of a miser, in real life he was quite generous. It seems that Benny had just refused to accept a check for performing at a charity event, but asked, 'But just in case I was accepting the money, how much was I refusing?' "*

For a list of possible amusing situations, see the chart at the end of this chapter.

Use Self-Effacing Humor

Another way you can show your sense of humor is to recount a funny episode that happened to *you*. Telling a story about how you handled an embarrassing or an awkward situation is a powerful communication tool, both in social and business situations. When you laugh at yourself, you convey confidence and poise. Maybe this is why so many successful speakers, entertainers, and business leaders use this form of humor to build rapport with their audiences. A modest amount of self-effacing humor shows you are not oversensitive about your weaknesses or past mistakes. When you can poke fun at yourself, you are telling everyone that you feel comfortable and confident.

The following are good examples of how some famous people poke fun at themselves:

A story attributed to Albert Einstein:

> *"I was at a young friend's home and he proudly showed me his eighteen-month-old son. I held the boy and gave him a big warm smile. The infant looked up at me and suddenly broke into a howl that shook the walls. I patted the little guy on the head and said fondly, 'You're the first person for years who has told me what you really think of me.' "*

Ava Gardner is rumored to have said this about herself:

> *"Deep down I'm pretty superficial."*

A telegram from Groucho Marx to the exclusive Friars Club in Hollywood:

> *"Please accept my resignation. I don't want to belong to any club that would accept me as a member."*

In a humorous moment Dolly Parton remarked:

> *"You'd be surprised how much it costs to look this cheap."*

The Three Biggest Mistakes to Avoid When Using Humor

1. Sexual and ethnic jokes and jokes about the disabled are inappropriate and can offend.
2. Sarcastic humor, if unchecked, alienates and offends because people take it personally.

3. Practical jokes can lead to accidents and be the kiss of death for a budding career.

Kicking the Shyness Habit Pays Off Fast

You might think that "old habits die hard," but with practice you can quickly change how you react and feel in social and business situations. Writing your own script of constructive "self-talk," sharing your expertise with others, and using your sense of humor can do wonders to boost your confidence. While in the past you often felt uncomfortable meeting new people, now you will know how to overcome shyness and make every conversation an enjoyable and rewarding experience.

AMUSING SITUATIONS THAT LEAD TO LAUGHS

Everyone has embarrassing or amusing moments that they can share with others. To help you remember a few funny stories, consider this list of common situations that may lend themselves to humorous retelling.

- A case of mistaken identity
- A mistaken telephone call
- A mix-up in gifts
- A family get-together
- An event at work or at school
- An event at the beach or in a pool
- An important meeting
- An unusual birthday party celebration
- What happened with an article of clothing
- A first day on the job
- An event in a fitness class
- A faux pas at a hotel or restaurant
- A blind date
- A most embarrassing moment
- An event described in the news
- Something your child or pet did
- A time when you were trying to be sophisticated
- An event that is funny now, but wasn't when it happened

part two

■

Speaking
in
Social
Situations

4
■ Mastering the Art of Small Talk

"I tell you right out I'm a man who likes talking to a man who likes to talk."

—SYDNEY GREENSTREET TALKING TO HUMPHREY BOGART
IN THE FILM *THE MALTESE FALCON*

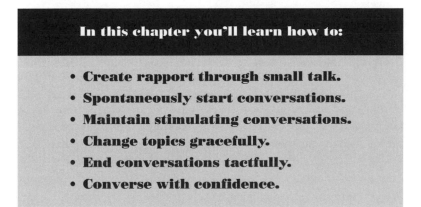

In this chapter you'll learn how to:

- **Create rapport through small talk.**
- **Spontaneously start conversations.**
- **Maintain stimulating conversations.**
- **Change topics gracefully.**
- **End conversations tactfully.**
- **Converse with confidence.**

Franklin Roosevelt, the thirty-second President of the United States, believed that most people were poor listeners, especially when it came to making small talk. Every so often, to prove his point and amuse himself, he would greet houseguests with, "I murdered my grandmother this morning." The usual response was a puzzled yet polite nod of approval. However, one evening a guest greatly impressed him when she smiled and said, "I'm sure she had it coming."

Small Talk Creates a Friendly Atmosphere

Small talk is light and casual conversation that avoids obscure subjects, arguments, or emotionally charged issues. If you are like many shy people, you might think small talk is a waste of time, but nothing could be further from the truth! Making small talk is an easy way to get to know someone, create a positive first impression, and gain self-confidence.

Discussing general-interest subjects such as movies, music, theater, sports, books, food, travel, and such demonstrates to others that you are approachable and friendly. When you offer a few light-hearted comments or ask and answer questions, you send the message that you are ready, willing, and able to communicate. This is especially critical for other shy people who look for a "green light" or extra encouragement before they even consider participating in a conversation. When you make casual conversation, other shy people will conclude that you are a person with whom they can easily converse.

Small Talk Allows for an Informal Exchange of Basic Information

One highly useful aspect of small talk is that it enables two people to learn a great deal about each other in a short amount of time. Small talk provides an opportunity for you to casually find out where people are from, what they do for pleasure and profit—even what they love to eat or what their lifelong dreams are. In addition, if you listen carefully, you will discover that most people readily reveal the topics they want to discuss or subjects in which they are interested.

When you hear an interesting remark, acknowledge it with a comment and an easy-to-answer follow-up question. For example, if an acquaintance mentions a recent vacation, you might respond, "I know exactly what you mean about traveling because it's one of my hobbies, too! What made you decide to visit . . . ?" Small talk is a confidence-booster because it enables you and your conversational partner to quickly find areas of common interest and helps you choose topics that both of you feel comfortable discussing.

Ten Steps to Mastering Small Talk

Have you ever wondered how some people can enter a roomful of strangers and strike up a conversation with practically anyone? Even if you are shy, the secret to pulling off this communication coup is easy if you follow these ten steps.

Step 1: Before the Event, Identify Several Interests and Experiences That You Are Willing to Discuss

"Be prepared."—Boy Scout motto

Can you imagine a marathon runner not warming up before a big race or an attorney improvising to the jury the key points of an important case? In each situation, preparation is the key to success. The same is true for mastering small talk. For the shy person, the first critical step in mastering small talk is preparing what YOU want to talk about. By identifying at least six or more "hot" topics and stimulating experiences, you can prime your conversational pump and get ready to communicate. To list possible topics, ask yourself questions such as:

"What have I read lately that I enjoyed or found thought-provoking?"

"What movie, play, or performance tickled my funny bone or captured my imagination?"

"What restaurants could I recommend to someone who shares my tastes in food?"

"What recordings or concerts have I heard that may interest other music lovers?"

"Where have I traveled that exceeded my expectations?"

"What new challenges am I setting for myself?"

"What are my current hobbies?"

"What plans do I have for this weekend or over the next holiday?"

"What insights can I share about my business or work that might be interesting?"

You may be reluctant to talk to strangers or previous acquaintances, but once you make this exercise part of your mental preparation for socializing, you will never be at a loss for words when the opportunity to converse arises. In addition, you'll discover many other people who share your interests and are willing to talk about what they enjoy.

H I N T: When you first meet a person, avoid these unpleasant, overly personal, or highly controversial issues because they can quickly degenerate into depressing conversations or arguments:

- Personal, health, money, or family problems.
- Divorce or death.
- Gory crimes and decaying moral values of Western civilization.
- Layoffs and gloomy economic predictions.
- Terrorism, war, pestilence, and famine.
- Emotionally charged issues such as abortion, welfare, or capital punishment.
- Sex, politics, and religion.

Step 2: Search for Individuals Who Seem Receptive

From the moment you enter a room, search for people who are already talking or appear as though they want to talk. These folks are usually the easiest ones to approach because they require little prodding to engage in conversation.

Step 3: Establish Eye Contact and Smile to Send Receptive Signals

Casual eye contact and a warm, friendly smile demonstrate your interest and desire to communicate. Eye contact for five to ten seconds indicates curiosity and is generally considered friendly. Take care not to stare at another person too intensely because this can make him or her feel uncomfortable. When the other person returns the eye contact, smile back. At that point you have made a connection and transmitted the message that you want to have a conversation.

This first contact is usually the precise moment when most shy people become nervous, fold their arms, and avert their gaze. Avoid "mixed signals" in which you make eye contact and then look away for several minutes. The other person often interprets this as a loss of interest. He or she may think that you looked and did not like what you saw.

H I N T: To neutralize your nervousness and communicate receptivity, unfold your arms, move your hands completely away from your face (including your mouth and chin), and smile. By keeping your body language open and relaxed, you'll send out confident and friendly signals that say you are available for contact.

Step 4: Be the First to Introduce Yourself and Ask an Easy, Open-Ended Question

Do you hang back and wait for others to start a conversation with you? The problem with this passive strategy is that the longer you wait, the more nervous and uncomfortable you will become. Instead, move into an action mode. Take the initiative and be the first to say hello. This not only demonstrates confidence and shows interest in the other person, but it gives you the opportunity to guide the conversation. Most people in social situations are perfectly delighted to chat if someone approaches them in an easygoing way. Begin your conversation by introducing yourself. Then follow with an easy-to-answer question about something in your immediate surroundings. In most cases, "open-ended" questions are best because they elicit detailed responses. The following are examples of open-ended questions that will encourage the other person to talk:

"How do you know our host?"

"What do you think of this spectacular view?"

"Could you explain to me how this . . . works?"

"What is your opinion of . . . ?"

"Why do you think . . . happened?"

You can also launch a conversation by offering a sincere compliment with a follow-up question or by making a lighthearted comment. As a rule, the earlier you introduce yourself in a conversation, the better. When you come to a pause in your conversation, smile, make eye contact, shake hands, and say, "By the way, my name is . . ."

H I N T: Be aware of cultural differences in what is considered a comfortable communicating distance. For most people and cultures, a span of about three feet between new acquaintances is about right.

Step 5: Listen Carefully for the Other Person's Name and Use It in the Conversation

> *"I don't remember anybody's name. Why do you think the 'dahling' thing started?"*—Eva Gabor

Even the most gregarious people often forget the names of the people they meet. The reason is that they are either thinking of what they are going to say next or are focused on making a good impression. For a shy person like you, mastering the ability to remember names quickly boosts your conversational power and really impresses the people you meet.

While I'm no memory expert, my ability to remember first names is good. Here is what I do to remember the first name of someone I've just met.

- At the moment of introduction I focus only on his or her name and face.
- I immediately repeat the person's name to make sure that I got it right.
- If I missed the name, I ask the person to repeat it.
- I quickly think of someone I know with the same name.
- I say the name periodically in the conversation.
- I always use the person's name when I close the conversation.

Step 6: Listen Carefully for Facts, Feelings, Key Words, Free Information, and Implied Statements

Another powerful tool to help you make small talk with strangers is active listening. Tune into facts, feelings, key words, free information, and implied statements that suggest topics of interest or common experiences. Listen for phrases or words that create a mental picture. For example, ". . . going on a dream vacation," ". . . excited about a new job," ". . . rescued an abandoned dog," "I can't wait to . . ." When you hear a word or phrase that triggers a picture, simply ask something like "You mentioned that you spent time in Chicago. What were you doing there?" or say "Chicago! That's where I grew up. How did you like working there?"

Listening Between the Lines Tells You What NOT to Say

When listening "between the lines" you may hear implied statements that suggest emotionally charged topics to avoid. Since many people often reveal their feelings unconsciously and indirectly, listening is your primary tool for knowing what and what not to say. If a person implies or states a negative feeling about a particular topic, avoiding that topic is probably wise. For example, in a social situation if I heard someone I had just met say any of the following comments, I would quickly change the subject to something more positive:

"After the jerks I worked for fired everyone in our department . . ."

"I couldn't wait to get out of that lousy marriage, so I . . ."

"You want to know what I really hate?"

"Don't get me started!"

Step 7: Disclose Some of Your Background, Interests, and Experiences

If you only ask questions and never share anything about yourself, your contact with others will be more like interrogations than conversations. Therefore, it is essential to tell people about yourself. However, don't overwhelm people with your life story or list your accomplishments as if you were interviewing for a job. Casually pepper your conversation with a bit of your background and experience and you will reveal who you are in a positive and interesting way. For example:

"When I was growing up in . . ."

"In my spare time I enjoy . . ."

"One of my favorite things to do is . . ."

"I spent about ten years working for a big company before starting my own business."

"I've been working as a . . . for many years."

H I N T: Let the other person know of any interests or experiences that you think you may have in common.

Step 8: Explore the Other Person's Interests by Encouraging Him or Her to Talk

Revealing information about your hobbies, job, or family makes it easy for others to know what you want to talk about. However, you do not want to prattle endlessly about yourself. Keep small talk stimulating by changing topics at the right time. This is effortless if you have made a point to listen for facts, key words, free information, feelings, and implied statements. Simply say, "I heard you mention earlier . . ." or "It's funny that you brought up that subject. I'm interested in that, too." Or you can merely change the subject by inquiring, "Do you mind if I ask you about something you mentioned a few minutes ago?"

H I N T: While discussing a variety of issues and subjects is desirable, bouncing around too much from topic to topic is annoying. If you do leave a topic before you or the other person is finished, just pick up where the two of you left off by saying, "Getting back to what you were saying before . . ."

Step 9: Highlight Mutual Interests

It may sound obvious, but one way to overcome shyness is to spend more time talking with people you like. Unfortunately, many shy people fail to cement the bonds with the likable people they meet in social situations. That is why emphasizing areas of commonality and mutual interests is important. For example, you can say:

"It's always good to meet someone who is interested in . . ."

"I'm happy I've finally met another alumnus of . . ."

"I love it when I meet someone who is as excited about . . . as I am."

"It's rare that I meet a person who enjoys . . . as much as I do."

Step 10: Restate Something You Found Interesting in the Conversation and End with an Invitation to Meet Again

Everyone agrees that the first few minutes of contact are important, but many fail to understand that the last moments of a conversation are equally crucial. Follow this format for ending conversations, and you'll leave a positive impression on the people you meet.

First, say a few words about an interesting topic that the other person discussed. Then add that you've enjoyed the chat. Look at the person, smile, shake hands, and use his or her name. Finally, if you are so inclined, suggest that the two of you talk again soon. Offer your business card or telephone number. Then ask the other person how you might reach him or her. The following example shows how to end a conversation the right way and leave a positive impression:

"Pat, it was really fun talking about the mystery you are reading. By the way, I belong to a mystery book club where a small group of us sit around and talk about what we've been reading. If you are interested in meeting some other mystery buffs, I'll let you know the time and place of our next get-together. [Look for a nod, smile, and agreement to this invitation.] How can I get in touch with you? Great! Well, talk to you later. Bye."

H I N T: Keep your farewells short. Even if the other person does not accept your invitation, that's okay—it's still worth suggesting a future meeting, for you may not get the opportunity again.

DOS AND DON'TS FOR MAKING SMALL TALK

Do:

✔ Make sure people are interested in a topic before talking too much about it.
✔ Stick to upbeat subjects.
✔ Balance the amount of talking and listening.
✔ Find out what other people enjoy discussing.
✔ Be willing to talk about subjects that you know little about.
✔ Reintroduce yourself to an old acquaintance.

DON'T:

✗ Indulge in endless shop talk or industry gossip when non-industry people are present.
✗ Gossip about the other guests.
✗ Stay in one area or speak only to one person.
✗ Look over a person's shoulder as you talk to him or her.
✗ Make negative snap judgments about the people you meet.
✗ Expect other people to carry the conversation.

5
■ Mixing and Mingling at Parties

"Comes New Year's Eve, everybody starts arranging parties. I'm the guy they got to dig up a date for."

—ERNEST BORGNINE FROM THE FILM *MARTY*

In this chapter you'll learn how to:

- **Prepare conversational topics for parties.**
- **Psych yourself up to meet new people.**
- **Enter a party and start talking with anyone.**
- **Join conversations already in progress.**
- **Enjoy meeting people and socialize with confidence.**

As Louisa May Alcott's fame grew, the American author of *Little Women* and supporter of women's suffrage frequently found her celebrity status tedious. Once while Alcott was mingling at a social event, an ardent admirer introduced herself and gushed, "If you ever come to Oshkosh, your feet will not be allowed to touch the ground: You will be borne in the arms of the people. Will you come?" Without batting an eyelash, Miss Alcott answered, "Never!"

Ask Who Else Is Attending the Event

Do you sometimes feel out of place at parties because you don't know anyone or never know what to say to the other guests? Most people are uncomfortable when they enter a roomful of strangers. However, you can do several things to make socializing at parties easier and more fun.

I recently attended a semiformal dinner at a fancy restaurant where I knew not one person, including the host. Normally, that would be a highly nerve-racking situation, but our savvy host made our mingling much easier by sending each of us a guest list which included a few words about everyone attending the dinner party. For example, among the guests was a former governor of New Jersey, a psychologist, several authors, and a demographics analyst. Armed with these nuggets of information, I did a little research about some of the guests. As a result, I felt much more confident and comfortable at the party, especially while we socialized before dinner.

Mixing and mingling at business and social get-togethers is easier if you know who is attending and a little something about them. I'm not suggesting that you spy or pry into anyone's personal affairs, but you can gather some interesting background information about their interests, hobbies, businesses, or recent experiences. For example, your host might tell you that one guest recently renovated his basement, that another is a budding artist about to exhibit at her first show, and that a third person volunteers at a youth center.

For a shy person those first awkward moments of contact at a social event can be torture, but some prior knowledge about the other guests' interests can facilitate conversations. About a week before the event, call the event's host or sponsor and ask him or her the following questions:

> *"Who are some of the other guests?"* (Knowing who is attending the event can ease party jitters and help you prepare for conversations.)

> *"Can you tell me a little about a guest or two whom you think I might like to meet?"* (The purpose of this question is to find which other guests you might enjoy chatting with because you share some common interests or experiences.)

> *"What does . . . like to talk about?"* (If you want to meet someone in particular, this question can help you uncover topics that he or she may be interested in discussing.)

"Would you introduce me to . . . ?" (This question lets your host know that you would like a formal introduction.)

Let your host know that you appreciate his or her efforts. End your telephone call with a thanks and comment such as "I'm really looking forward to seeing you and meeting the other guests."

C A U T I O N: In case it is unclear, be sure to ask your host if your invitation also includes a date or a friend.

A Little Research Pays Off

Now that you know something about the other guests, it's time to go to work. With a little reading, you can probably research enough information to carry on a conversation about a few subjects that you know are "hot button" topics for your fellow guests. Let your own curiosity and interest be your guides about how much time and effort you devote to researching a particular topic. For example, perhaps your host tells you that one person who will be at the party has recently returned from a trip to China. First, look at a world atlas or encyclopedia to find the major cities, then get a general idea of the geography and some basic information about the country. Or check the public library's *Reader's Guide to Periodic Literature* for recent magazine or newspaper articles on China. You can even go online to get some updated information. When you meet this person, you could confidently say:

> *"Fran mentioned that you just returned from an exciting trip to China. I just read an interesting article in* National Geographic *about two Americans who traveled through China by bicycle. I'd love to hear a little about your trip. What was it like where you traveled?"*

Many people volunteer their time and talents for special causes or organizations. If you discover that a guest volunteers his or her time for a certain charity, make a telephone call to research the services or benefits it provides the community. Ask about any recent media reports that have highlighted its achievements. Then after you meet the person, refer to the organization by saying, for example:

> *"Jamie told me that you volunteer at the children's hospital. I read in the newspaper about the work that volunteers do there and I found it very inspiring. What kinds of things are you doing at the hospital?"*

Many of your fellow guests will probably be interested in either playing or watching sports. You can learn a lot about this popular topic by reading the sports page in your local newspaper. After you meet a "sports nut" you could say:

> *"Jack told me that you're a college football fan. I read that our local university has a pretty good team this year. Do you think they might make the top ten playoffs?"*

Where to Find Information

Whether the guest you're interested in volunteers at a local literacy program or teaches martial arts, find out what you can about the topic. Use these easily accessible resources:

- Peruse the papers, weekly magazines, and news shows for related topics.
- Ask your local librarian.
- Search computer services on the Internet, as well as America On-Line or Compuserve, for information about the subject.
- Refer to reference books that offer notes on a broad range of subjects such as:

  - *An Incomplete Education,* by Judy Jones and William Wilson (Ballantine Books)
  - *Benet's Reader's Encyclopedia* (Harper & Row)
  - *The Best, Worst & Most Unusual,* by Bruce Felton and Mark Fowler (Galahad Books)
  - *The Encyclopedia of New York City,* by Kenneth T. Jackson (Yale University Press)

- *The New York Public Library Desk Reference* (Prentice Hall)
- *The People's Almanac,* by David Wallechinsky and Irving Wallace (Doubleday)
- *The Way Things Work,* by D. Macaulay (Houghton Mifflin)

Psych Yourself Up

Going to a party where everyone is a stranger can be daunting. Soon after I moved into a new apartment, a neighbor invited me to a party. While I normally looked forward to meeting new people at parties, on this particular evening I felt nervous walking into a room where I knew only one person, the host. As I approached the door, I considered turning around and going home until I saw some other guests arriving. Then it was too late to bail out, so I took a half a dozen deep breaths and said these words to myself: "What is the worst thing that can happen? If I don't have a good time, I can always leave. Who knows, I might meet some interesting people!"

Make the "Butterflies" in Your Stomach Fly in Formation

Only you know how you really feel when you walk into a roomful of strangers at a party. Even if you are nervous, you can appear approachable and willing to talk. Be sure to enter the room smiling, establish eye contact, and nod. Say hello and introduce yourself to the people you meet and you'll be setting a friendly tone for conversation later.

Then find the host and present him or her with a small gift, such as a bottle of wine, an appetizer, or flowers. It is not how much you spend on the gift that is important, but the thought that shows you appreciate your host's hospitality. This is also a good time to ask your host if he or she needs help with any last-minute details. Believe me, your host will really appreciate your thoughtfulness even if everything is under control. And talking to your host will be a warm-up for conversations with other guests at the party.

Look for a Friendly Face and Start a Conversation

Your first mission at the party is to mix with the other guests. Do this by going to where the other guests congregate. The most common places are the food tables, kitchen, or the refreshment bar. Introduce yourself immediately to those around you and start a conversation with a light comment or easy-to-answer question. The following examples and explanations illustrate the dynamics of a typical conversation.

"Hi, I live down the street from our host. My name is . . . How do you know Jean?" (Free information and an open-ended question give both people an opportunity to establish how they know the party's host.)

"Jean and I met while walking our dogs. Are you an animal lover, too?" (This free information and closed-ended "fishing" question reveal an interest and a desire to learn more about the other person.)

"This dip is great. I had it once in a Greek restaurant. I think it's made with yogurt. Do you like it?" (While this closed-ended question requires only a short answer, it opens the door for more conversation based on food, cooking, or restaurants.)

"I love that necklace you're wearing. Those blue stones look fabulous with your great tan. Were you vacationing somewhere recently?" (A compliment followed by an easy-to-answer question show interest in the other person, while allowing the conversation to continue around travel and jewelry.)

"I don't know a soul here except Jean. Are you friends with the other people here?" (This disclosure shows trust by revealing what is an uncomfortable situation for many people. It also helps establish rapport between guests who are looking to meet new people and make friends.)

When it comes to starting conversations, it's not what you say, it's how you say it! Most people go to parties expecting a few questions to get the conversations going. Be sure that you are ready to answer some commonly asked questions, too.

Don't Be a Potted Plant—Keep Circulating

Mingling is a vital part of socializing at a party, so don't grow roots or stay parked in one part of the room for too long. A good rule to follow at a larger party is to circulate after ten or twenty minutes of conversation. Of course, looking at your watch and saying, "Time's up! Got to move on. Bye!" would be quite rude. Remember not to end your conversation abruptly, but wait for a slight pause or other appropriate time. Say you enjoyed the chat, use the person's name, and simply say you are going to circulate a bit.

Joining Conversations Already in Progress

Now that you've had a few successful one-on-one chats, it may be time to mingle and join a group of people talking. Egad! How in the world can you break into the conversation without being pushy or getting rejected? While many shy people see this as a difficult task, it is much easier than you might think. Follow these five steps:

Step 1: Look for an Open Group

When I go to a party, I always search for a group of people who are having a lively and upbeat conversation. These folks are easy to spot because they are the ones who are smiling and having fun. Their open body language says it all: *We are having a good time, so please join us.* These guests could be talking about books, movies, TV programs, or just about anything, but chances are humor is a fundamental part of their exchange. I enjoy these groups because they are talking about what interests me. Moreover, I go to parties to have fun, not to solve the world's problems. You, on the other hand, may prefer to discuss more penetrating or serious issues such as philosophy, political theories, or ethical values. In this case, look for an open group of people who are discussing similar topics by exchanging their ideas, feelings, and opinions, and not engaging in heated debates.

Step 2: Move Within Communicating Distance

Once you spot a receptive group, move to within four or five feet of them. Establish eye contact with the speakers; smile and show that you are interested in what they are saying. You might think that this is being a bit forward, or even nosy—and in a way it is—but that's

Open Group	**Closed Group**
O O	X X X
O O	X X
O ←←	X X X

Enter the group from here.   Look for another group to join.

okay. Remember, people go to parties to socialize and make new friends. Also, don't assume that the guests in the group all know one another. In fact, many have probably just met for the first time and don't even know one another's name. One warning, though: If you overhear what is obviously a personal or heated conversation, move away and look for another group to join.

Step 3: Show a Desire to Participate

Once you have established that the group is open, clearly show your desire to participate. When one guest makes a joke, be sure to smile and laugh along with the rest of the group. When someone else makes a striking comment, nod your head. Look for who appears to be the most friendly and open person in the group, because he or she will probably be most receptive to you.

Step 4: Ask a Question or Make a Light Comment

Now is the time for you to start talking. Simply ask a question or make a comment based on what you heard the group discussing. You might share some information or anecdote related to the topic. Hopefully, this will encourage a response or question from someone else in the group. Short of these techniques, you can always just ask, "Do you mind if I join you?"

Step 5: Introduce Yourself to the Group

Always introduce yourself to the person in the group who responded to you first, and then to the other guests. It almost never fails that the other guests will take your introduction as a cue to introduce themselves, if they haven't already. These introductions help make everyone in the group feel more comfortable. Make it a point to use the guests' names right away and refer to an earlier comment or question to restart the conversation. Take care not to talk too much, get confrontational, or make judgmental comments. Your goal is to establish rapport and have a casual and fun conversation. Keep an eye out for other guests interested in joining you. When you spot someone, open up a space for him or her and you'll make a friend immediately! Introduce yourself and the others in the group. When you use the names of the people you just met, you'll make a big impression! When you are ready to move on, shake hands with everyone, use their names, and say, "I enjoyed meeting all of you."

H I N T: Besides the tips in Chapter 4, "Mastering the Art of Small Talk," these additional suggestions will help you remember the names of people in a group:

- ☞ Slow down the introductions so you have an opportunity to concentrate on and repeat aloud each person's name.
- ☞ "Hook" the first initials of the names into short words or abbreviations. For example, if you just met, Ira, Bob, and May, think "IBM."
- ☞ Take a few seconds to recall the names of the people in the group.
- ☞ If you missed the name, listen carefully for someone else in the group to refer to the person by his or her name.
- ☞ When you hear the name again, repeat it to yourself and then refer to the person using his or her name.

Not All Groups at a Party Are Right for You

After you have had one successful conversation in a group, then move on to another. You'll discover that some groups are easier to mix with than others and are more to your liking. If your conversation doesn't go as well as you might have wished, that's okay. Perhaps it was the topic or the people in the group. No problem, just move on and try again. Soon you'll become quite proficient at spotting the groups at parties that are right for you.

THE TEN BIGGEST MISTAKES SHY PEOPLE MAKE IN PARTY CONVERSATION

When you avoid these common communication pitfalls, you'll boost your personal appeal and have a lot more fun at parties. The mistakes are:

1. Having a negative attitude and anticipating rejection.
2. Folding your arms and not smiling.
3. Remaining silent instead of being the first to say hello.
4. Breaking the ice with a dull question such as "What do you do?"
5. Replying with only one-word answers without revealing additional information or topics of interest.
6. Talking too much without asking questions or listening for "key words" or "free information" from other people.
7. Talking too little without showing interest or enthusiasm.
8. Not introducing yourself and not using the other people's names.
9. Arguing about minor details and being a know-it-all.
10. Ending the conversation abruptly or on a depressing subject.

6

■ Hosting a Get-Together That
Leaves Your Guests Talking

*"Written invitations should be addressed by name to the people ex-
pected to attend, even if that means doing a little research to find out
if that awful person your friend seems to be living with has a name."*
—JUDITH MARTIN, ALSO KNOWN AS "MISS MANNERS"

In this chapter you'll learn how to:

- **Calm pre-party jitters.**
- **Make your guests feel welcome.**
- **Introduce guests to one another.**
- **Help shy guests engage in conversation.**
- **Deal with "difficult" guests.**
- **Relax and enjoy your own party.**

Some time ago a shy friend invited my wife and me to a get-
together at his home. I was a bit surprised by the invitation because I know that socializing at parties makes him uncomfortable.
When I asked what prompted him to host a party, he responded,
"For me, one of the hardest things at parties is meeting a bunch
of strangers. So if I host the party and invite whom I want, then I
won't have that problem." As it turned out, his party was a great
success and he now finds attending other people's parties more enjoyable.

Host a Get-Together and Shed Your Shy Image

To a shy person, hosting a party may sound terrifying, but it can be one of the best ways to build social confidence and shed a "wall-flower" image. Ironically, a person who may feel reserved at someone else's party can be outgoing when he or she is the one hosting a get-together.

It's true that planning a party requires you to focus on the practical aspects, including choosing the right theme, food, music, and guests. But that isn't all you need to do. Experienced party givers agree that the secrets to a party's success rest in these elements:

- Making guests feel welcome.
- Encouraging lively conversation.
- Remaining relaxed and gracious.
- Attending to details that make guests feel pampered.
- Adding a few special touches that make your get-together memorable.

Dealing with Pre-Party Nerves

Tonight is your get-together and your guests will be arriving soon. Although you've planned and prepared your party as if you were a professional party giver, you still might feel nervous. Remember in Chapter 4, "Mastering the Art of Small Talk," you learned to focus your attention outward toward the people you meet and not to worry about goofing up. In addition, use these techniques to minimize any last-minute jitters:

☞ Find a chair and sit quietly with your eyes closed for a minute to gather your thoughts.
☞ Imagine your home filled with people having fun and enjoying one another's company.
☞ Look around your home and absorb the party atmosphere.
☞ Put on some relaxing music as you attend to the final details.
☞ Put yourself in a "party frame of mind" by smiling at yourself in the mirror.

☞ Don't worry if everything isn't perfect. Your guests won't notice or care if the scented soap in the bathroom doesn't exactly match your hand towels.

☞ Adopt an easygoing attitude so that you will appear gracious and relaxed.

Three Steps to Making Guests Feel Welcome

As a shy person, you know how tough it can be to attend a party—even when you know a few of the other guests. As a host, you can make those first few anxious minutes a lot more comfortable by helping your guests to integrate into the party area. Follow these steps.

Step 1: Welcome Your Guests Personally

Treat your guests as if they are the most important people in your home. Offer to take their coats or show them where they can put their things.

Step 2: Spend Time with New Arrivals

Bring your guests into the main party area and offer them some refreshment. Start a short conversation based on something light, such as an unusual appetizer you prepared for the party or a recent amusing experience. Ask them about something important in their lives, such as "How are the kids?" or "Are you settling into your new house?" or "How's your tomato crop coming along? I hope it's as good as last year's." The key point is to devote your full attention to the new guests, even if only for a few minutes. This adds a personal touch that makes them feel welcome.

Step 3: Help New Arrivals Mix with Other Guests

Introduce your new guests to the other people at the party. The shy guests will be particularly grateful if you help them over this hurdle. Before you introduce your guests, take a moment to consider what you want to say. Keep it upbeat and brief, and avoid professional titles or potentially embarrassing information. The best introductions include a personal connection and a bit of humor. For example:

"Folks, excuse me for a moment. I want to introduce you to two of my oldest and dearest friends, Ned and Stacey. We went to school together—and no, I won't say how many years ago. Ned and Stacey, this is . . ."

"Bill and Carol, I'd like you to meet Diana. Diana just moved here from Columbus, and since all your kids are in the same school, I thought that you might like to get to know each other."

A few tips on introductions: Etiquette varies, depending on the group, age, and culture, but these basic rules always apply.

- Introduce men to women.
- Introduce younger people to older people.
- Introduce subordinates to superiors.
- For most informal parties, introduce guests by their first names. (You may wish to include last names for more formal or social/business get-togethers.)
- Clearly say the name of each guest and allow an extra moment for them to greet and shake hands.
- If possible, add a few words about the people so they have an easy way to start conversations.

Encouraging Entertaining Conversation Between Guests

Along with introducing guests to one another, a good host stimulates entertaining conversation. This is where revealing your guests' interests can help other shy people feel more comfortable and enliven the party atmosphere. Helping guests to mix and mingle is easy if you keep moving through the party and introducing them to one another, particularly those who share common interests. Interject a comment or open-ended question that allows your guests to talk about their "hot buttons" or unusual experiences. For example:

"Bev, I've been meaning to ask you about living in Fairbanks, Alaska. It sounds so exciting! What's it like living in America's last frontier?"

"Gosh, John, it's been a long time! How's the import-export busi-ness faring these days?"

"Ellen, tell us that funny story about the time your kids . . ."

"Rich, you use the Internet a lot. What have you found that's the most interesting?"

"Trude, you've got to tell us the funny thing that happened when your dachshund Romeo got out of the house at five A.M. to chase after a female German shepherd."

Easing Out of the Conversation

Once you get people talking, spend a few minutes enjoying their company and conversation. You can then gracefully slip out of the conversation by saying:

"Well, I can see you folks have lots to talk about. Excuse me while I go check on the refreshments."

"I hear some new guests arriving. Excuse me for a moment."

"Don't mind me. I need to slip away to ask someone something."

"Excuse me. I'm going to get something to drink. Can I get any-one anything?"

Keep an Eye Out for "Difficult" Guests

As you move through the party and chat with your friends, keep your eyes open for anyone having a problem with a "difficult" guest. It could be two people arguing, a bore trapping another guest in a cor-ner, or someone overindulging. In any case, one guest's inappropri-ate behavior can make the rest of your guests feel embarrassed and uncomfortable. As the host, you're the one your guests will look to to remedy the situation. The following "conversational crisis man-agement" techniques can help keep difficult guests from spoiling your party and leaving you holding the bag.

Defusing an Argument

Discussing and exchanging different opinions at parties can be stimulating and entertaining, but some people (particularly if they have had too much to drink) may forget that arguments are inappropriate. If you hear a discussion heating up to the critical point, don't wait until tempers boil over. Quickly step in to calm everyone down and change the topic. Believe me, the guests will thank you for saving everyone from an embarrassing scene. To tactfully defuse the situation, use the guests' names and say something like:

> *"Les. Micky. Hold it a second. I think this discussion is getting a little too intense. After all, this is a party—not the war tribunals for the Security Council. Let's change the subject to something a little lighter. Les, I understand your kids' soccer team is playing in the city championship next week."*

> *"Gail. Tim. I'm calling a time-out on this discussion. I know you're both very passionate about this subject, but I'd really appreciate it if you would just agree to disagree—at least for tonight. Say, Tim, planning any trips in your RV this summer?"*

Rescuing a Guest from a Bore

Everyone knows the uncomfortable feeling of being trapped by the tedious person who reveals the endings of books and movies, tells long-winded stories, discusses his or her latest medical malady, or pumps other guests for free professional advice. As the host, it's your job to rescue a guest from a bore's clutches. Here is how you can do it gracefully:

> *"Sorry to interrupt you two, but I need Steve's help for something. He'll be back in a few minutes."* (Then the rescued person can get "conveniently" distracted by another guest.)

> *"Phil, sorry to interrupt you and Beth, but I want to introduce you folks to some people. They're over here. Come on."* (Introducing the bore and trapped guest into a larger group makes it more difficult for a blabbermouth to monopolize the conversa-

tion. Plus, the now-freed guest can excuse himself or herself more easily from the conversation.)

"Fred, do you mind if I steal Jane away from you? I need her help in the kitchen, RIGHT NOW! Jane, it's time for you to heat up those wonderful-looking appetizers you brought." (Asking the bore for assistance allows the trapped guest to go free.)

"Paula, please do me a big favor tonight and spare us the details of your latest operation. We're going to eat dinner soon and I don't want to spoil anyone's appetite." (This direct and honest approach may be necessary for those particularly difficult guests who can't think of anything else to talk about but themselves.)

"Larry, why don't you call Kate at her office about that problem? She's here to have fun and not talk about your taxes! Kate, I hear that you and Paul adopted a baby. How do you like being new parents?" (Unless this is a networking situation, the trapped guest will appreciate your intervention.)

A final tip on dealing with difficult guests: An assertive approach is best when confronting a guest who engages in any kind of inappropriate behavior. Be friendly but firm. Ask to speak with the person privately in another room. Then briefly define the problem behavior and ask him or her to stop.

Hosting a Party Is Fun and a Great Confidence-Builder

It takes a lot of work and planning to host a party, but the payoffs are worth it! Your creativity and sense of fun will enliven your get-together. Your guests will have a great time and will see you as a caring and outgoing person who knows how to entertain at home. Helping your guests mix and knowing that you can handle any unexpected problems that may arise will boost your confidence tenfold. You may still be a little reserved at other people's parties, but as the host in your own home, you will shine all evening.

Fifteen Tips for Enjoying Your Own Parties

1. The more you prepare ahead of time, the more you will enjoy your party.
2. Consider a theme. It enlivens parties and gives the guests something to talk about.
3. Guests are the most important part of any get-together. The more diverse the group, the greater the opportunities for spontaneity and fun.
4. Invite people who you think will mix well together.
5. Let your guests know the arrival time, proper attire, what to bring, and, if necessary, the time you are sitting down to eat.
6. Pay equal attention to all your guests.
7. Always have more than enough food and refreshments on hand.
8. Distribute food in various locations so guests can circulate, nibble, and talk.
9. Add an extra touch of class with flowers, candles, and scented soaps.
10. Have a variety of music, including dance and easy listening.
11. Be flexible and prepared for the unexpected spill or broken wineglass.
12. Once the doorbell starts ringing, stop preparing and enjoy your guests' company.
13. Don't engage in frantic or nervous cleanup until after the party.
14. When everyone has left, have a drink with a friend and toast to a wonderful night of fun and entertaining.
15. Relax, smile, and have a great time. After all, it's your party!

7

■ Talking Your Way Out
of Toxic Conversations

*"I do not want people to be agreeable, as it saves me the trouble of
liking them."*

—JANE AUSTEN

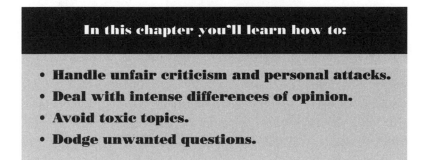

In this chapter you'll learn how to:

- **Handle unfair criticism and personal attacks.**
- **Deal with intense differences of opinion.**
- **Avoid toxic topics.**
- **Dodge unwanted questions.**

A shy student from one of my communication classes recalled an
unpleasant conversation with her mother-in-law. "Don't you think
that Kevin Jones is really a loud, obnoxious person?" sneered the
mother-in-law. Taken aback but not tongue-tied, the daughter-in-
law assertively replied, "Betty, you may not realize it, but Kevin is
one of my oldest and dearest friends and I really don't appreciate
comments like that about him." The mother-in-law gulped in embarrassment and quickly changed the subject.

Beware of Conversational Traps!

Do you remember the last time you attended a party, family gath-
ering, or business meeting and got trapped into a toxic conversation? The awkward situation probably started innocently enough

as a "friendly exchange of ideas." Then, with lightning speed, a barrage of stinging words or personal comments caught you off guard. You thought that a brusque retort would put an end to it, but that only encouraged the loudmouthed lowbrow even more. By the time you realized that you had "taken the bait," the aggressive lout had sprung his conversational trap and delivered the verbal coup de grâce. You languished in public humiliation while the boor gloated over his triumph and your embarrassment. The question is, How can you avoid becoming a victim of a conversational bully and escape a toxic conversation with your self-esteem intact?

Don't Overreact—Do Stay Calm

If you find your conversation heading for a confrontation or argument, keep your cool so you can find a way to change the topic. Remaining calm shows confidence, and it gives you time to think of an appropriate response. The biggest mistake you can make in responding to a personal attack or unfair criticism is to "shoot back with both barrels." Fighting back verbally shows the other person that he or she has hit a nerve, and now you are in for a real battle. Once an aggressive person identifies a vulnerable spot, he or she will keep picking at it until you give in or lose your temper. On the other hand, if you don't react to a provocation, you offer nothing for the conversational shark to feed on.

Don't Argue—Do Listen

Shy people are particularly attractive targets for conversational bullies who like to draw unsuspecting individuals into a verbal fray. Remember, bullies love to argue and win because it makes them feel more important when they dominate others. If someone challenges you, don't react. Instead, hold your ground and ask an open-ended question. This stalling strategy gives you time to develop a response that allows you to find an exit. The following examples show how to stand up to a verbal bully and deflect a personal attack without getting sucked into an argument.

Quarrelsome boor: *"It is people like you who are ruining our country!"*

Shy person: *"Excuse me?* (Looking surprised) *Are you talking to me?"*

Quarrelsome boor: *"You're darn right I'm talking to you!* (Wagging a finger in your face and getting louder) *You and your disgusting people have really made a mess of our country and it's about time we good folks did something about it!"*

Shy person (in a calm, firm voice): *"I agree, our country has problems, but I'm not sure exactly what you are talking about. Could you be more specific?"*

Quarrelsome boor (getting worked up and moving closer): *"You know exactly what I mean! You ought to be ashamed of yourself!"* (Casting the bait)

Shy person (ignoring the insult and in a cool, confident voice): *"Actually, I still have no idea what you are talking about.* (Frustrating the boor by not taking the bait and forcing him to start over again) *What are you trying to say?"*

Quarrelsome boor (reaching the boiling point with no one to fight with, he pulls out all the stops): *"You [blankity blank-blank] people always play dumb, but you know darn well what's the matter with this country and you're it! Why, if it were up to me, I'd . . ."*

Again, don't respond to the attack, no matter how tempted you may be. Displaying a cool aloofness shows you are in control and you are not going to fall into his or her trap. Conversational boors usually give up and look for someone else to harass when their provocation fails to get reactions. If, however, the boor persists, then excusing yourself from the conversation is perfectly acceptable.

Shy person (acknowledging the boor's irate behavior and setting the stage for a polite exit): *"I'm sure you have your reasons for getting so upset, but I still don't understand what you are trying to say. If you'll excuse me, there's someone else I'd like to say hello to. Good-bye."*

"Let's Agree to Disagree"

Fortunately, not every discussion or difference of opinion ends in an argument. When there is a mutual exchange of ideas, many people enjoy broadening their understanding of an issue. However, when debating emotionally charged issues, you and someone else with vastly different values or opinions will probably never agree. If left unchecked, this volatile situation can escalate into a toxic conversation that can permanently damage a relationship.

For example, you may support a local legislator whom your conversational partner despises. Both of you know that neither of you will change your opinions. In fact, the more you argue, the more tightly you will cling to your individual positions. However, you can show you are listening and understand the key factors influencing the other person's viewpoint while clearly exercising your right to disagree. These examples show how to politely disagree.

> *"I understand that you see our city's economy going down the tubes because of the local plant closings. Nevertheless, I also see small businesses expanding in other areas that will make our city less dependent on one large employer, and I think that is good."*

> *"From what you say, it's clear that you don't think our city has a bright future, but I can't think of anywhere else I'd rather live."*

> *"I know you disagree with me, but I liked our mayor because . . ."*

Change the Topic Before Emotions Escalate Out of Control

To avoid saying something that both of you will later regret, you can redirect the conversation to a less inflammatory topic. Don't wait until emotions and voices reach a fever pitch to end the discussion.

In a firm and friendly voice say, "Since we're not going to change each other's minds, let's just agree to disagree. By the way, how is your vegetable garden coming along this year?"

Dodging Unwanted Questions

Since you have a right to privacy, you are under no obligation to provide an answer just because a busybody asks you a personal question about your finances, political persuasion, family matters, or health. To discuss or not to discuss and how much to reveal is your choice. Never reveal information that you prefer to keep private. Use these techniques to evade snoopy inquisitors and avoid toxic topics.

Technique 1: Provide a Vague Answer and Ask a Question

This technique deflects unwanted questions with answers that provide little or no specific information. Asking a question in return throws the conversational ball into the other person's court.

For example, if a nosy in-law asks: *"How much money do you make?"*
You can say: *"I make enough money to keep me happy. How are you getting by in these tough times?"*

If an office gossip asks: *"Is it true all they say about your new boss?"*
You can say: *"My new boss and I get along just fine. How is your part of the project coming along?"*

If a prying neighbor asks: *"That new car must have cost a bundle. How much was it?"*
You can say: *"I paid a fair price. Do you want the dealer's name where I bought it?"*

If a competitive sibling teases: *"I'll bet your love life is on the rocks again. Am I right?"*
You can say: *"The jury is still out. I'll keep you informed."*

Technique 2: Refuse to Answer and Change the Subject

This technique suggests that the question is unwelcome and that you are not going to answer it. Changing the subject offers both people a diplomatic way out of a sensitive situation.

> For example, if a snoopy boss asks: *"What do you do all weekend by yourself?"*
> You can say: *"I prefer to keep my personal life private. When do you want the Jones file?"*

> If a competitive coworker asks: *"How much was your raise?"*
> You can say: *"I'd rather not say. By the way, how's your job search going?"*

> If a client asks: *"How did you vote in the last election?"*
> You can say: *"I believe in the barbers' old saying, 'I discuss anything but politics and religion.' By the way, I've been meaning to ask you where you bought your computer."*

Technique 3: Refuse to Answer and Discourage More Questions

This technique makes it absolutely clear that the question is "out of bounds." A follow-up word or two helps discourage persistent or aggressive people who may try to take advantage of a personal relationship to gain private information.

> For example, if a competitor asks: *"What has XYZ Inc. invested in recently that I won't read in the papers?"*
> You can say: *"Please don't ask me questions like that. My clients' financial investments are confidential."*

> If a meddling friend asks: *"So what did Sal tell you that was so hush-hush?"*
> You can say: *"You know I don't tell my friends' secrets. That's why you and I are still friends."*

Make Silence Work for You

Dealing with confrontations and toxic topics is not always easy, and pushy people can drive you to the breaking point. Whenever that happens, pause for a moment, take a deep breath, and say nothing. A short period of silence can defuse nosy or aggressive people because they will not know what to do when you do not react to their taunts. Then when you are ready, respond in a way that maintains your integrity, self-respect, and, above all, composure. When silence is the appropriate response, follow this advice: No reply is best.

EIGHT TIPS FOR AVOIDING TOXIC CONVERSATIONS

1. Stay cool and never let conversational bullies make you lose your temper.
2. Don't feel that you have to defend yourself or respond to accusations.
3. Change the topic before you get trapped into an argument.
4. Ignore nasty comments or verbal attacks—it drives bullies crazy!
5. Use your sense of humor to defuse a potential argument.
6. Avoid people who like to play the "devil's advocate." They are just looking for victims.
7. Never go on the attack in a toxic conversation.
8. Get away from toxic conversationalists as quickly as possible.

8

■ Presenting a Toast to Friends and Family

"Happiness is good health and a bad memory."

—INGRID BERGMAN

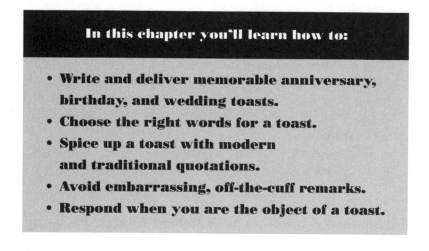

In this chapter you'll learn how to:

- **Write and deliver memorable anniversary, birthday, and wedding toasts.**
- **Choose the right words for a toast.**
- **Spice up a toast with modern and traditional quotations.**
- **Avoid embarrassing, off-the-cuff remarks.**
- **Respond when you are the object of a toast.**

William Lloyd Garrison was a nineteenth-century American abolitionist who was accustomed to answering insults from hostile audiences. However, when the British Anti-Slavery Society toasted Garrison at a banquet in his honor and presented him with a gift, the articulate speaker grew silent. "If this had been a rotten egg," he finally responded, "I should have known what to do with it, but as it is a gold watch, I am at a loss for words."

"We Want You to Make a Toast"

Oh, no! At the last minute your best friends ask you to give a toast at their wedding reception. They know that you're shy, but do they realize that you would rather endure dental surgery without novo-caine than stand up and speak before a group? You can't insult them by saying no, so you reluctantly accept the honor. The only prob-lem is, you have no idea what to say and the big day is tomorrow! What are you going to do?

Good Toasts Make Joyous Occasions Even More Special

You can do one of three things when you make a toast at a special event such as a wedding reception, birthday, or anniversary party. First, you can mumble a few benign words that fall flat as a pancake. Second, you can "wing it," risking an inappropriate comment or slip of the tongue that will embarrass everyone—and especially you! Or third, you can impress everyone with a few choice words that will enhance the special occasion. If you want your words to remain in everyone's hearts and minds—and have fun, too—follow these steps to prepare, practice, and give your toast.

Step 1: Identify the Audience

As in all public speaking, knowing your audience and the envi-ronment in which you are going to speak increases your confidence and helps you decide what to say. To that end, find out the follow-ing information:

- Who will be present? (This information helps you choose ap-propriate quotations and anecdotes for your toast.)
- Is it an intimate celebration or a large formal affair? (Informal and personal toasts are welcome for small family celebrations. A traditional toast plays better for a larger, more formal occasion.)
- Is the event being held inside or outside? (If the event is going to be outside, you may have to practice your toast at a louder vol-ume so everyone can hear your "pearls of wisdom.")
- Will you need a microphone? (If you don't test the microphone before offering your toast, it will undoubtedly fail or will squeal so loudly that it will blow the ears, hats, and toupees off the guests.)

- Who else is giving toasts and when is your turn? (Knowing your position in the lineup of toasts gives you an opportunity to mentally prepare for your big moment.)

Step 2: Choose Words That Show Acknowledgment and Appreciation

For shy people, the good news about speaking before a group is that the best toasts are short, simple, warm, and personal. Toasts can be funny or heartwarming, and are always optimistic. Start by consulting the many excellent quotation books listed in the bibliography. You can also find inspiring lines at your nearest greeting card shop and even inscribed (not painted!) on the walls of libraries and public buildings. Draw on your favorite movies, television shows, poems, novels, and even buttons with printed slogans for poignant words that put a little "spice" in your toast. Usually, though, the best source of inspiration is your personal experiences with the person or people you are honoring.

Step 3: Write Out and Practice Your Toast

Shy people take note! Professional speakers know the importance of the first few moments of a speech, so they write, memorize, and practice their opening lines until they can say them flawlessly. Ad-libbing or failing to practice a toast, especially if you are inexperienced, have had a little too much to drink, or are nervous, can lead to an embarrassing moment. Consider the husband who made this unfortunate slip of the tongue. After one too many glasses of champagne, he toasted his wife at their fiftieth wedding anniversary party by saying, "Here's to my petty wife!" Oops! Obviously, he meant to say "pretty," but no matter how much he apologized, the damage was done. The moral of the story is to know what you are going to say and rehearse it aloud at least five times before you make your toast. You won't be sorry.

A few words of caution: Always anticipate how individual audience members might react to your words *before* you say them. If you are not sure your words are appropriate, they probably are not. IF YOU HAVE ANY DOUBT, LEAVE THOSE QUESTIONABLE WORDS OUT!

Step 4: Make a Last-Minute Check

The big day has arrived and your time to speak is a few minutes away. You have chosen your words with care and have practiced your delivery. Although you're still a little nervous, conscientious preparation increases your confidence and poise. Now is the time to do a last-minute check.

- Silently rehearse your toast, focusing especially on the first and last sentences.
- About fifteen minutes before you speak, make a short trip to the rest room to check your appearance, gather your thoughts, and practice your toast again.
- Make funny faces in the mirror and blow air through closed lips to relax your jaws.
- Make clenched fists and then open your hands to help you relax your muscles.
- Take a drink of warm water and quietly clear your throat.
- Take a few deep breaths to calm your jitters, return to the group, and wait for your turn.
- When you receive your cue, stand up, pause for a few seconds to plant your feet, smile, and look at your audience.
- Gaze with admiration at the person or people you are about to toast.
- Speak loudly enough so everyone can hear.
- After the toast, nod to and smile at your audience before you sit.

Toasts for Special Occasions

The following occasions often call for toasts. Review the examples of traditional and contemporary quotations below and choose the kind that best suits your occasion. You can draw upon them to create your own toasts. Remember, some are heartfelt, others are humorous, but all must be sincere.

Toasts for Anniversaries, Engagements, and Weddings

Happy memories and an optimism about the future are the key ideas to focus on for these joyous occasions. Begin a wedding anniversary toast by taking a trip down memory lane. Make the past come alive by using words that describe the music, movies, or events that reflect the couple's experiences. Then forecast a rosy and rewarding future. For example:

> "I would like to propose a toast to our good friends Diane and Terry on their fiftieth wedding anniversary. When this happy couple tied the marriage knot, they listened to the swinging sounds of Glenn Miller on the radio and danced the jitterbug at Roseland Ballroom in New York City. Now on this happy occasion, please help me wish them many more wonderful years together and say that their best dance is yet to come."

If appropriate, you can adapt a humorous quotation to fit an engagement toast. For example, I attended a wedding at which one guest drew on Mae West's words for inspiration. He lifted his glass to the bride and groom and began his toast with the following:

> "Mae West said, 'Marriage is a great institution, but I'm not ready for an institution!' Well, if Mae West had the bright future that this happy couple has before them, she would have been committed a long time ago."

Quotes About Love and Marriage

Here are some more words and phrases that can help spice up toasts about love and marriage.

> "Why does a woman work ten years to change a man's habits and then complain that he's not the man she married?"
> —Barbra Streisand

> "Don't marry a man to reform him—that's what reform schools are for." —Mae West

> "Marriage is a mistake that every man should make."
> —George Jessel

"Love is a flower that turns into fruit at marriage." —traditional

"A man in love is incomplete until he is married. Then he is finished." —Zsa Zsa Gabor

"It's like olives, dear. It's something you acquire a taste for." —Maid discussing marriage with a newlywed in the 1961 film *Lover Come Back*

Making a Birthday Toast

Birthday toasts are simple and fun. The main points to emphasize in the toast are gratitude, affection, friendship, good health, and the future. One easy way to personalize your toast is to describe some significant events in the year of the person's birth based on his or her interests. Then use words related to this interest to show your appreciation. You can use almanacs, encyclopedias, and special-interest books to find fun facts about practically any subject or hobby. For example, to toast an ardent baseball fan, you might say something like:

> *"Our friend Dean was born on this day in the year 1953. That year the New York Yankees won the American League pennant for the fifth year in a row. In that same year, baseball voted Dizzy Dean into the Hall of Fame. In fact, our birthday boy got his name from this great pitcher and we appreciate all he has done for our team. So let's raise our glasses and wish a very happy birthday to Dean, a great guy, who is definitely number one in our hall of fame."*

You can also share an anecdote that exemplifies the person's character. For example:

> *"I want to share just one reason why I think Pam's picture should illustrate the word* friend *in the dictionary. It was last winter when I called on Pam to . . ."*

Quotes About Birthdays and Age

Adapt quotes such as these to add some good-natured humor to your toast.

"You are only as old as you feel. By the way, has anyone seen my Geritol?" —adapted

"The old pearl-oyster produces the pearl." —Chinese proverb

"It takes about ten years to get used to how old you are." —unknown

"Old age is when your liver spots show through your gloves." —Phyllis Diller

"Old age is not for sissies." —unknown

"Old age is like flying a plane through a storm. Once you are aboard, there is nothing you can do." —Golda Meir

"I smoke cigars because at my age if I don't have something to hang on to I might fall down." —George Burns

"The secret to staying young is to live honestly, eat slowly, and lie about your age." —Lucille Ball

Toasting Family and Friends

Reunions, parties, and holiday dinners frequently call for toasts. Use words like *lasting friendships, loyalty, fond memories, togetherness,* and *good times together.* Talk about *humorous times, unforgettable experiences,* and *tender moments.* These words describe the stuff of close relationships. Avoid any mention of past arguments or disagreements. Then wish everyone many more happy times together. Here is an example of a humorous toast at a holiday reunion of high-school friends:

> *"I propose a toast to our group of friends and all the great times we have shared. I promise I will not mention any names like . . . or make any incriminating statements such as . . . After all, I want to save all of you the embarrassing explanations to your spouses later! What I will say is that I love these annual reunions and reminiscing about the many unforgettable experiences we have shared over the years. May our friendships continue to grow year after year."*

A toast to family members often focuses on appreciation and personal challenges. You can also use gentle humor to poke a little fun at parents, siblings, and relatives.

"No one said it was going to be easy growing up with two English teachers in the family. And were they right! That is, I mean 'correct.' But, I can truthfully say that I owe everything I have accomplished to my family because they taught me these three important lessons: First, 'Native ability without education is like a tree without fruit.' Second, 'Do what you love and the money will follow.' And finally, to quote George Burns, 'Happiness is having a large, loving, caring, close-knit family—in another city.' "

Quotes About Friends and Family

Words such as these can interject humor and warmth into your toast.

"A father's goodness is higher than the mountains; a mother's goodness is deeper than the sea." —Japanese proverb

"You can choose your friends, but you only have one mother." —Max Schulman

"A man can't get rich if he takes care of his family." —Navaho saying

"Being popular is important. Otherwise, people might not like you." —Mimi Pond

"Friendship is an arrangement by which we undertake to exchange small favors for big ones." —Baron de Montesquieu

"If Harvey said it to me once, I bet he's said it, oh, probably a million times, 'Mr. Dowd, I would do anything for you.' " —James Stewart about his invisible rabbit friend, in the 1950 film *Harvey*

Toasts Make Your Relationship Special

Offering a toast at a birthday, wedding, or family get-together is an honor that even a shy person like you can enjoy. When you take the time to choose, practice, and present the right words for a toast, everyone will see you as a confident speaker. But even more important, your friends and family will cherish your words long after the celebration is over.

THE FLIP SIDE OF A TOAST: A GRACEFUL RESPONSE

The King of England once described what he did while his subjects sang "God Save the Queen." He said, "I try to look dignified, but under no circumstances do I join in." Follow these other dos and don'ts when you are the object of a toast.

Do:

✔ Remain seated with your hands folded in your lap or on the table.

✔ Say "Thank you" and, if you wish, add a few words of appreciation.

✔ Wish everyone the same happiness they wish for you.

✔ Drink only after others have finished toasting you.

Don't:

✗ Drink to yourself.

✗ Pick up your glass until the toast is over.

✗ Feign modesty by claiming unworthiness.

✗ Recite a tedious list of people you want to thank.

9

■ "Telebonding" Your Way to Personal Relationships

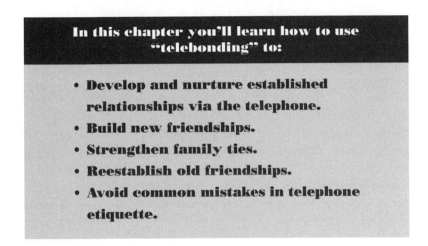

In this chapter you'll learn how to use "telebonding" to:

- **Develop and nurture established relationships via the telephone.**
- **Build new friendships.**
- **Strengthen family ties.**
- **Reestablish old friendships.**
- **Avoid common mistakes in telephone etiquette.**

Dorothy Parker, the American theater critic and short story writer, was famous for her irrepressible humor and play on words. Once while attending a party she said, "Excuse me, I have to go to the bathroom." After a moment, she continued, "I really have to use the telephone, but I'm too embarrassed to say so."

Telebonding Helps Build New Relationships

Telebonding is the process of developing, nurturing, and enhancing new and close relationships via the telephone. Perhaps you met someone on vacation or at a convention who you would like to get to know better. The bad news is that you and the other person live in different cities or states. The good news is that you exchanged telephone numbers and that there is a real possibility of establishing and maintaining a long-distance relationship.

Even if you are shy, you can initiate a new telebonding relationship by phoning the other person. It is helpful to have a "reason" for the call and then build the conversation around that subject area. To begin you can begin say something like:

> *"Hello, is this Sandy? This is Joe Catlin. We met last week at the New York City Dog Show. I'm the guy who lives in Chicago and you told me you had just adopted a dachshund. I hope I haven't called at an inconvenient time. The reason I'm calling is to say how much I enjoyed meeting you and to give you the information about the dachshund newsletter I promised you. By the way, how is your new puppy?"*

Take care not to chat for too long or, on the other hand, to cut your conversation short: About ten to twenty minutes on your first call is sufficient. If the other person responds enthusiastically to your call, you can say, "I enjoyed talking with you. Would you mind if I called you again?" If the answer is yes, you have started the telebonding process. Sure, it takes some nerve for a shy person like you to call a stranger you've only met once or twice, but think of what you have to gain.

Telebonding Helps Maintain and Nurture Established Friendships

Do you have an old friend who lives halfway across the country whom you see only once a year, at best? Why let the distance keep you apart? Don't be shy about calling often. Telebonding allows you to maintain existing relationships that otherwise might whither and die. For example, my wife and one of her college friends rarely see each other, but have had weekly telephone conversations for years. Their friendship continues to grow and they are even closer now than they were twenty-five years ago. When they do see each other, it is as if they have been talking face-to-face all the time they were apart. This is telebonding at its best!

Telebonding Helps Bring Family Members Closer Together

Did you move away from home and over the years lose touch with your parents, siblings, or other relatives? Telebonding is an ideal way to reestablish family ties and build stronger personal bonds. For example, when I moved away from home, my sister and I rarely called each other. Although we enjoyed the time we spent together during the Christmas holidays, the only other time we spoke during the year was for our obligatory birthday telephone calls. After several years of this pattern of communication, I noticed our relationship was becoming more distant. Then my sister and her husband suggested that my wife and I join them on a vacation. As the frequency of our telephone calls increased, so did the quality of our relationship. Now we talk at least once or twice a month! Once again, telebonding enhances a personal relationship that was in danger of disappearing.

Telebonding Is a Way to Reestablish Old Friendships

If you haven't called a friend or family member in a while, the conversation may take a little extra time to get going. The exchange may feel awkward at first, especially if there are short periods of silence. You may feel tongue-tied and want to hang up, but stay cool and keep on talking.

To feed the conversation, ask easy-to-answer open-ended questions and listen for key words, free information, and implied statements. As the other person speaks, listen for the topics that he or she seems to want to talk about. At the same time, be sure to share plenty of free information of your own so the other person will know what you want to talk about. "Icebreakers" such as these can help get the conversation going:

"I can't believe it's been so long since we spoke last. Let's catch up with what each of us is doing."

"How are things going with your kids and the family?"

"Are you still working at . . . ?"

"Have you heard from . . . (a mutual friend, parent, associate, etc.)?"

"How's that project you were working on progressing?"

"I want to share some good news with you."

Telephone Etiquette

There are right and wrong ways to talk on the telephone. The following ten tips for telephone etiquette will enhance telebonding with your conversational partner and help you overcome your initial shyness.

Telephone Etiquette Tip 1: Always Identify Yourself When You Call

As unbelievable as it may sound, there are some adults who still play the childish telephone game "Can you guess who this is?" My usual response to this lame way to start a telephone conversation is a simple "No, should I?" If that poor excuse for a telephone introduction isn't maddening enough, some people launch into a long story the moment the other party answers the telephone. Most people need a few moments to recognize even the most familiar voice on the telephone when a call comes unexpectedly. That's why when my mom calls, she begins the conversation with, "Donnie dear, this is your mother!"

Always begin a telephone call by identifying yourself. You might say:

> *"Hi, this is . . ."* Or *"Hello, my name is . . . You may remember that we met last week at . . ."*

Telephone Etiquette Tip 2: Ask Whether You're Calling at a Convenient Time

Most people agree that an unannounced visit to a friend is generally considered rude, yet many people do just that when they call and assume that the person they are calling is available to talk. Many people don't even consider that their call may come at an inconvenient time. That is why it is important to understand that the telephone is the "electronic doorway" to the home. Whether the person you are calling is a new friend or family member, it is just good manners to ask, "Is this a good time to talk?" Or "Have I got you in the middle of dinner (a meeting, another phone call, feeding the baby, etc.)?" This gives the person you are calling an option to talk now or return your call at a more convenient time. If he or she is busy or unavailable, simply ask, "When would be a good time to get back to you?"

How to Say, "Now Is Not a Good Time for Me to Talk"

If you are shy, you may feel reluctant to tell a friend or acquaintance that he or she is calling at an inconvenient time. It is perfectly all right to say, "Bill, I'd love to talk to you, but I'm right in the middle of dinner (just getting ready to leave, watching my favorite TV show, etc.). Can I get back to you in about an hour or so?" Then it is up to you to return the call when it is convenient. If this is an acquaintance, you may want to ask, "By the way, what's your telephone number again?"

Telephone Etiquette Tip 3: Avoid Screening Your Telephone Calls

Many shy people with answering machines now screen their calls before answering the telephone to avoid inconvenient interruptions or unsolicited sales pitches. If, however, you always screen your calls, it can give the impression that you are unavailable, asocial, or uncomfortable talking on the telephone. Answer your telephone unless you have a good reason not to, such as when you are working, eating, or sleeping.

Telephone Etiquette Tip 4: Don't Keep Two People on the Line

Call Waiting is a service that allows you to receive a second call while you are already speaking to someone on the telephone. However, Call Waiting can cause offense if you put the first person on hold while you talk to the second caller.

Here is a good rule to follow if you receive a second call: Put the first call on hold for no more than forty-five seconds. Any longer than that is just plain rude. You can say to the second caller, "I'm on the other line right now. Let me get back to you in a few minutes or ..." However, if it is vital that you take the second call, then quickly go back to your first caller and say something like "I'm sorry to cut you off, but I need to take this call. Can I call you back in about an hour?"

Telephone Etiquette Tip 5: Don't Just Complain About Your Problems

When you call a friend, you might want to talk at length about your problems. While venting some frustrations during a telephone conversation with a friend is okay, going on too long can inhibit tele-bonding and put a strain on the relationship.

After complaining about your difficult boss, irritating neighbor, or prying in-law, share some positive experiences as well. Change the conversation by saying something like "Well, I guess I've been grumbling about my ... long enough. Say, I forgot to tell you that I've signed up for a course that's given on the Internet." Or shift the conversation to your friend by asking, "What's new with you?"

Telephone Etiquette Tip 6: Ask About Events in the Other Person's Life

Shy people often hesitate to ask questions because they don't want to appear nosy or too personal. Ironically, friends get offended when you *don't* ask them questions about the major experiences in their lives. The reasons are simple: Friends like to talk about themselves, and they usually want to share intimate details with those they trust. This is what telebonding is all about.

Show interest by asking the other person about the important events in his or her life. This shows that you care and helps to build rapport and trust. The following examples illustrate how to encourage your friend to talk about important aspects of his or her life:

> *"So how did your big discussion with your boyfriend (parents, boss, etc.) go?"*

"The last time we talked you said you were thinking of changing careers. What's going on with your job?"

"I'm eager to hear how your class reunion went. Tell me all about it."

Telephone Etiquette Tip 7: Don't Criticize or Make Judgmental Statements

When your friend complains endlessly, you may feel like saying, "Quit sniveling, you wimp!" or "If you had listened to me in the first place, you wouldn't be in this mess!" The tendency to criticize and make harsh comments about a friend's behavior, predicaments, or decisions—even if they are well intentioned—can inhibit telebonding and damage a relationship.

Avoid offering advice unless someone asks for it. Then, present your words of wisdom sparingly and tactfully. Consider posing questions such as "What are your options?" or "In a perfect world, what would you do?" The point here is not to advise, but to be a good listener and help your friend find his or her own solutions.

Telephone Etiquette Tip 8: Avoid Dwelling on Negative Topics

True, unhappy personal relationships, complicated economic theories, or a rehash of the world's problems are legitimate topics of conversation, but when discussions get bogged down in these heavy topics for too long, it can get to be a bit too depressing. And if you are guilty of dwelling on negative topics, the other person may feel trapped and not be too enthusiastic about your next telephone call.

Provide some relief and use your sense of humor to show you can keep these issues in perspective. The best telebonding occurs when both people can share a laugh with each other. Change the topic of conversation to something that both of you can feel good about. You can say something like:

"Well, I guess I've gone on long enough about that. Why don't we talk about something more pleasant? Do you have any plans for the weekend?"

Telephone Etiquette Tip 9: End Your Conversation on a Positive Note

As in face-to-face conversations, if you end your telephone contact without warning or on a negative note, it leaves the other person feeling uncomfortable. When this happens, he or she may feel less inclined to talk with you the next time you call. Telebonding increases when you find some aspect of the conversation that you can rephrase in a positive way. Repeat what you liked about the exchange and conclude your telephone conversation in a warm and enthusiastic way. For example:

> *"Though we live miles apart, when we talk on the telephone I feel like we are roommates again."*

> *"It's always great talking to you. I'll give you a call next week to find out how your job interview went. Good luck!"*

> *"Thanks for listening. It's great to have a best friend like you."*

> *"I love talking with you when I feel blue because you always make me laugh."*

Telephone Etiquette Tip 10: Initiate Your Share of the Calls

Good relationships are based on give-and-take, and telebonding is no different. If you always wait for your friend or family member to place the call to you, then you may be giving the impression that the contact is not that important to you. On the other hand, if you are the one who always initiates the telephone call, then you might be the one who feels slighted. If the cost of the long-distance telephone call is an issue, then discuss it openly. There are many long-distance calling plans that make telebonding quite economical. Besides, if you lived in the same town and went out to lunch with your friend once a week, you would probably spend far more than the cost of a long-distance call. What is more important is that each party in a long-distance relationship make a fair share of the telephone calls. When this happens, the telephone can enhance your relationships.

Telebonding Builds Relationships Across the Street, City, or Country

Most shy people want more contact with the people they care about because it makes them feel good and fulfills a need for intimacy. Whether you want to develop a long-distance romance, chat with an old friend, or build bonds with a family member, telebonding will improve your ability to communicate. The next time you want to share some good news or just have a conversation to discuss the latest news, call a friend and watch your relationship grow.

THE TEN BIGGEST MISTAKES IN TELEPHONE ETIQUETTE

Taking telephone communication for granted can lead to embarrassing moments and hurt feelings. Avoid these common mistakes and your telephone relationships will soar.

1. Not identifying yourself when you call.
2. Assuming you are calling at a convenient time.
3. Constantly screening your calls.
4. Keeping two people on the line at once.
5. Only talking about your problems.
6. Not asking about the important events in other people's lives.
7. Criticizing or making judgmental statements.
8. Dwelling on depressing subjects.
9. Ending your conversation abruptly.
10. Not calling on a regular basis.

■

part three

Speaking
in
Business
Situations

10
■ Interviewing Your Way to a New Job

"Of course I'm the man for the job. What is the job, by the way?"
—PETER O'TOOLE AUDITIONING AS T. E. LAWRENCE IN THE FILM
LAWRENCE OF ARABIA

In this chapter you'll learn how to:

- **Start the interview with a prepared introduction.**
- **Make a positive first impression.**
- **Avoid getting stereotyped as shy.**
- **Clearly communicate your greatest skills and strengths.**
- **Make your body language and voice exude confidence.**
- **Quietly "blow your own horn."**
- **Handle embarrassing and trick questions.**
- **End the interview with a shot at the job.**

Like all Hollywood hopefuls at the beginning of their film and dance careers, the elegant Fred Astaire had to take a screen test. The response was, "Can't act. Slightly bald. Can dance a little."

Write Your Own Script

Today is the day of that all-important job interview and you don't want to say the wrong thing or get tongue-tied. You are hopeful because you have a professional-looking résumé and lots of experience, but when you enter the company's office, you discover that three other applicants are also interviewing for the position. How is the interviewer going to decide who gets the job? The fact is that résumés only get you the interview, not the job. Your demeanor plays a vital role when you sell yourself and your skills to the interviewer. If he or she stereotypes you as "shy," you might as well kiss your chances of getting the job good-bye!

Avoid Being Stereotyped as Shy—Be Ready with a Prepared Introduction

Studies show that you have less than five minutes to make a positive and memorable impression on the interviewer, so you need to know what you are going to say. When shy people get nervous, they typically clam up or ramble about where they went to school and what jobs they have held.

To avoid these pitfalls, present a concise introduction that tells the interviewer three of the most important points about you. Explain clearly how your skills can make things easier for the company and save them money. This example shows an effective response to a typical opening question such as "Tell me about yourself":

> *"I want you to know three important things about me. First, I have more than twenty years' experience in marketing and sales in high-tech medical equipment. Second, over the years my clients have included many major hospitals and research facilities in this country. Third, since I have an economics degree and understand the budget requirements of the health-care business, I can help clients set up equipment purchasing plans that are beneficial to them and profitable for your company."*

Communicating Confidence Is Your Competitive Edge

Webster's Ninth New Collegiate Dictionary defines confidence as "a state of mind marked by easy coolness.... Confidence stresses faith in oneself and one's powers without any suggestion of conceit or arrogance."

Do you exude confidence or do you let your shyness show when you interview for a job? Can you clearly answer questions or do you fumble for the right words? Most people do not include the ability to express themselves clearly on their résumé. However, your communication savvy can convince an interviewer that you are the right person for the job.

The interviewer has many questions about your abilities, experience, and communication skills. Can you clearly describe and back up your proposals? How do you react under pressure? Do you shy away from or embrace competition? Are you a team player? Can you skillfully deal with difficult clients and associates? The way you conduct yourself during the interview will help answer these questions and give your interviewer valuable insight into your abilities. In other words, communication skills help show that you are up to the job.

Open Body Language Shows Poise

Shy people often unconsciously reveal a lack of confidence through their closed body language. Never forget that it is not just what you say, it is how you say it. Step lively, keep your head up, have friendly eye contact, smile, and offer to shake hands as you enter the interviewer's office. After you take a seat, sit forward slightly in your chair and wait for the interview to begin. Be aware that the interviewer is probably observing your body language during the short period of silence while "looking" over your résumé. Keep your body language open, with your arms unfolded and your hands away from your face. Now is a good time to mentally review the points you want to make about yourself and the questions you want to ask during the interview. Once the interview begins, you may periodically "mirror" the interviewer's open body language. This will help build rapport between you.

Your Persuasive Voice: Moderate Volume + Enthusiasm = Confidence

Do you remember the last time you were at a job interview and the interviewer asked you to repeat your answers because you were speaking too softly? Nothing reveals nervousness more than a soft, quivering voice or monotone. Along with your body language, the tone of your voice reveals a great deal about your confidence and is a powerful selling tool. When you introduce yourself, speak in a moderate volume and with plenty of enthusiasm. Enunciate your words and use the tone of your voice to emphasize words that you want the interviewer to remember most. Before your interview prepare at home; use a tape recorder to practice your prepared introduction and build your vocal confidence. Or practice introducing yourself to a friend or family member. Remember that practice will make you feel more confident and comfortable during your interview.

Communicate Your Abilities and Achievements

Shy people often refrain from talking too much about themselves, but a job interview is no time to be modest. To be seriously considered for a position, you need to express your achievements in an unaffected and straightforward way. No one will know just how good you really are at what you do unless you tell them. A glowing testimonial letter or two from a past client or employer doesn't hurt either. In other words, it is okay to gently "blow your own horn," as you learned in Chapter 2. Do not hesitate to state your accomplishments and their benefits to past employers without exaggerating their impact. If the interviewer is unfamiliar with the technical aspects of your previous jobs, use familiar words instead of abbreviations, acronyms, or jargon, and resist the temptation to go into complicated explanations.

Ask Questions to Uncover an Employer's Needs

Why should an employer give you a job? Just because you are an attractive person and competent is not a good enough reason. You must emphasize that the employer or business will benefit by hiring you. To sell yourself, you need to discover the employer's specific needs. Then, and only then, can you convince the interviewer that you are the right person to fill the position.

Exactly how do you find out what the employer needs? Simple. Ask questions. Use the local library, chamber of commerce, or newspapers to research the industry as a whole and the company where you're interviewing in particular. Then ask informed questions that incorporate the information you have found. Not only does this demonstrate that you know something about the company, but it also persuades the interviewer that you are confident and well-informed. For example, you can ask:

"I read recently in a trade magazine that ... How is your company planning to deal with these kind of changes over the next year?"

"What are your company's top priorities for the next year?"

"What is your biggest challenge in the accounting (sales, editorial, etc.) department?"

"In what ways would you like to see things change in your company over then next few months?"

Asking questions allows you to indicate your interest in the company, cover points that the interviewer doesn't bring up, and display knowledge of the industry.

Tell How Your Skills Can Benefit the Employer

How will an employer benefit from hiring you? You must be able to answer this question, even if the interviewer doesn't ask it directly. If you dwell on long detailed explanations without highlighting how your skills will benefit the interviewer's company, then you will be communicating only half the message. Shy people who work as professional engineers, accountants, lawyers, computer engineers, scientists, and in other technically oriented positions frequently make this mistake during job interviews.

For example, during a job interview, an exceedingly bright but shy computer engineer explained the features of a particular software program at great length. Finally the interviewer interrupted to ask, "It's obvious that you know a lot about computers and such, but how can you help our company increase its profit?" To you, the value of your skills may seem obvious, but do not assume others share your perspective or understanding. Tell them what you can do and how they will benefit. The following examples illustrate how to tie your skills and achievements to the needs of a potential employer:

> *"As an experienced office manager, I can help this company meet its future cost-cutting goals by using support staff and office space more effectively."*

> *"With my extensive experience as a telemarketing trainer, I can show new sales reps how to save time by qualifying leads before they go out on sales calls."*

> *"As an associate with XYZ Attorneys-at-Law, I brought in several new small-business clients to the firm and believe I could do the same thing here."*

Handling Embarrassing and Trick Questions

"So why *exactly* did you get fired?" is the kind of stressful question that can leave anyone—especially a shy person—flustered and tongue-tied. The trick to dealing with stressful questions is to anticipate them and prepare your answers ahead of time. Expect questions relating to your on-the-job performance, but don't feel that you must answer illegal or inappropriate questions about your health, family, or other personal issues. While most interviewers ask legitimate questions to assess your skills, some may make improper inquiries or set verbal traps to see how you respond under pressure. If an interviewer asks you negative or hostile questions, be ready to reply with a positive statement about yourself. Never repeat negative statements. In your reply, be sure to include free information that reinforces your special strengths whenever possible.

Be prepared for stressful questions, inappropriate questions, or even illegal questions, but remember that your goal is to move on in the interviewing process and get a job offer—not alienate the interviewer with an angry response. Here are several examples:

Question: "Has an employer fired you from a job?" A legitimate "testing" question. Don't repeat the word *fired*. Answer briefly without going into detail or making excuses and then quickly bridge to a positive point.

Answer: "Once I was let go from a job because I didn't have the necessary computer skills. Since then, I have become proficient in several word-processing programs."

Question: "Why have you held so many jobs?" This is a legitimate question. Be candid but brief when you reply. Focus on your accumulated experience and tie it to what you believe the interviewer wants in a job applicant.

Answer: "It's true that I have had a variety of employment experiences over the past two years, and I've learned a lot from each. I'm interested in the marketing position with your company because I'm looking for the one job that allows me to combine my sales expertise, economics background, and love of high-tech media."

Question: "What have you been doing between jobs?" This is a legitimate question. Emphasize the skills you have to offer the employer.

Answer: "Beyond continuing my job search, I have been upgrading my business writing and computer skills. Plus, I volunteer my time at a local community organization, teaching their staff how to increase their donations through better use of their computer mailing lists."

Question: "What was your biggest failure on the job?" This is a negative question designed to test your confidence. Rephrase the question, offer a short answer, and bridge to a positive statement.

Answer: "I suppose I was most disappointed when I didn't get promoted to district sales manager, but since then I have gained more experience dealing with the technical side of sales and marketing."

Question: "Why do you want to leave your present job?" This is a legitimate question. Be candid but brief. Repeat the skills you have to offer and connect them to the job you seek.

Answer: "I wanted more challenge and responsibility. I find that I'm very good at supervising people who are working in a team situation. That's another reason I'm interested in the job you're looking to fill."

Question: "Why do you want to change departments? Don't you like your supervisor?" Answer the first question. Ignore the second one. It's a trap.

Answer: "I think that by transferring to the marketing division, I can use my knowledge of the product and my sales skills to help the company increase its customers' satisfaction."

Question: "You're not wearing a ring. Why isn't a good-looking person like you married?" You do not need to answer this question, but take care not to alienate the interviewer. He or she may just be inexperienced. This may be a good time to ask the interviewer a question.

Answer: "I prefer to keep my personal life private. But I'd like to hear more about your company's policy on providing additional training for their employees."

Don't Raise Any "Red Flags"

Some shy people may mistake an interviewer's inquisitiveness as a signal to "reveal all" about an unpleasant employment experience. Tempting as it may be, avoid negative comments about past bosses, coworkers, or employers. Negative comments raise "red flags" for interviewers and may suggest that you have a hard time working with others. Never make comments such as:

✗ *"You wouldn't believe the lousy conditions where I used to work."*
✗ *"My boss and I had a difference of opinion on what I was supposed to do."*
✗ *"The managers at my last job didn't know what they were doing."*

✗ *"I got fed up because all my coworkers did was gossip and dump their work into my lap."*

✗ *"You've never met a lazier bunch of supervisors."*

Eleven Questions to Ask About the Position and Salary

Shy people often forget that they have a perfect right to ask the interviewer certain questions about the jobs they seek and company policies. In fact, you are interviewing them as much as they're interviewing you! Preparing a list of questions will build your confidence for when you reach this point in the interview. What do you want to know about the job you are interviewing for? If the interviewer did not cover the following questions, you are entitled to bring them up before the interview concludes. You will eventually want answers to questions such as:

"What is the salary range for this position?" (You may not want to ask this first off, but don't wait until the final interview to find out the salary doesn't meet your financial requirements.)

"When would I start?"

"What is included in your benefits package?"

"Can you describe the opportunities for advancement?"

"What are the specific responsibilities and time requirements of this job?"

"About how much travel does the job require?"

"Who would be my direct supervisor?"

"Who are the people I would be working with?"

"When do you plan on deciding who gets the job?"

"When can I expect to hear from you?"

"Will you notify me even if I'm not chosen for the job?"

Sum Up What You Have to Offer

End your interview the same way you began it. Tell the interviewer the three most important things you want him or her to remember about you. Sell yourself as a congenial, skilled professional who meets deadlines and works within budgets. Emphasize that you are flexible, can consistently produce desired results on time, and work well with others. In addition, align your goals with those of the company. Remember that the only reason an interviewer will even consider hiring you for a job is that you've convinced him or her of your capacity to help the business succeed in its financial goals or mission.

Seek "Closure" by Asking for the Job

The interview is nearly over and you have given it your best shot. You have confidently summarized how you can benefit the company. You have answered the interviewer's questions clearly and candidly. Now is the time to thank the interviewer for the opportunity to tell about yourself and do one more thing: ask for the job.

To a shy person like you, it may sound pushy, but every successful salesperson knows that to get the sale you need to ask for it. Since you are selling yourself, the best way to emphasize that you want the job is to simply ask for it. The following examples show how to thank the interviewer and ask for the job:

"I want to thank you again for the opportunity of talking to you. Based on what you've told me, I am very interested in the position. Now, let me ask you this question. From what you've learned about me today, do you think that I am a good candidate for this position?"

"Thank you for the interview. I hope you consider me for the position because I think I can help your company reach its goals. What would you say my chances are of getting the job?"

Sometimes, but not always, a direct question can elicit a job offer on the spot. After thanking the interviewer, you can ask:

"Do I get the job?"

You may or may not get offered the position, but after this interview no one could ever accuse you of being shy!

BLOWING YOUR OWN HORN

If you don't blow your own horn, no one will do it for you. The following examples show the wrong way and right way to let others know about your achievements.

WRONG WAY	RIGHT WAY
"I was the best sales rep in my department." (too general)	*"I increased repeat sales by twenty-five percent in two months."* (specific example)
"I reconfigured a flextime INS program for the virtual office workstations that ran upgraded applications of DOS." (too much jargon)	*"I developed a computer program that allowed our staff at home to use the same software as our staff in the office."* (easy-to-understand language)
"I can draw just about anything on a computer." (too general)	*"I have used a computer program to design car parts."* (specific skill)
"There's nothing I don't know about this business." (empty boasting)	*"Even with ten years of experience, there's always more to learn."* (knowledgeable, but willing to learn)

11
■ Leading a Meeting with Confidence

"When it comes to authority, he who holds the thread holds the ball."
—PROVERB

In this chapter you'll learn:

- **Ways to build your confidence when leading a meeting.**
- **Ten rules for better meetings.**
- **How to handle difficult people in a meeting.**
- **Dos and don'ts for great meetings.**

I once worked for a manager who appeared serious and shy most of the time. His conversations with the other writers and editors were usually short and all business. However, when he held our weekly department meeting, it was as if someone turned on a switch and this man came to life. From the moment he began the meeting, he punctuated his vigorous agenda with jokes, stories, and laughs. While we did not think of him as a great conversationalist, he has a reputation for running terrific meetings.

"You Want Me to Lead the Meeting!?"

Oh, no! Your boss has just asked you—the shyest person in your office—to organize and present the department's weekly staff meeting.

As you see yourself before an audience of your peers, subordinates, and supervisors, your stomach does a double back flip with a twist. How are you going to keep your knees from knocking and your voice from quivering? What are you going to say and how in the world are you going to handle some of those wild characters in your department who love to give the person leading the meeting a hard time?

Standing in front of your coworkers and taking charge can be scary, but if you know how to handle it, leading a meeting can build your confidence and give your career a big boost. Even if you are shy, you can impress your peers, subordinates, and supervisors if you know the three secrets to leading a productive meeting: being well organized, sticking to your agenda and timetable, and keeping control of the group. The following ten rules for better meetings will help you to lead a meeting with confidence.

Ten Confidence-Boosting Rules for Better Meetings

Rule 1: Set Your Objectives

Clearly defining four or five objectives for your meeting builds self-confidence because it clarifies your goals, thus making them easier to achieve. To help articulate your meeting objectives, ask yourself questions such as:

"What information, ideas, decisions, issues, or problems do I need to address in this meeting?"

"How do the objectives for this meeting match the broader objectives of our department?"

"What is the exact purpose of this meeting and what must I accomplish?"

"How do I want people to feel when they leave the meeting?"

Rule 2: Prepare a Written Agenda and Timetable

When you know your objectives and about how long it will take to accomplish each one, you are in control of the meeting. By preparing a written agenda with a minute-by-minute timetable, you can judge if your meeting goals are reasonable within the allotted time. If you conclude that the agenda is unrealistic or too high-pressured, then make your schedule adjustments before the meeting. Covering a few important meeting objectives thoroughly is more productive than speeding though six or seven major issues with only cursory comments. The more meetings you lead, the more confident and skilled you will become at estimating how long various issues will take to cover. A simple agenda might look something like this:

MEETING AGENDA

Time: 10:00–10:45 A.M.

Day: Monday

Objective: Collect ideas for summer charity event

10:00–10:10: Welcome everyone to the meeting; highlight agenda and objective.

10:10–10:15: Make brief announcements.

10:15–10:30: Split into three individual groups for short brainstorming session.

10:30–10:40: Report from group leaders on each group idea (five minutes each).

10:40–10:45: Conclude with a few words about meeting the objective and a thank-you to the participants.

To show others that you are well prepared, distribute the agenda a few days before the meeting. This informs people of the meeting's purpose, gives them time to prepare, and allows them to plan their other tasks around it. While flexibility in running the meeting is essential, sticking with your agenda and timetable shows you are well organized and is an important confidence booster.

Rule 3: Invite the Right People

"Not another boring meeting!" is often the cry of people who do not belong at a meeting in the first place. What could undermine your self-confidence more than forcing everyone in a department to attend a meeting where only a handful participate? Instead, boost your credibility by inviting only the people who need to attend the meeting and can make some contributions. You can always send a memo or E-mail to the people who did not need to attend but need to know the results. To determine whom to invite, ask yourself:

"Is there a more efficient way to use John's time than by having him attend this meeting?"

"Will Jan's contributions help to achieve the meeting's objectives?"

"Can we reach our meeting objectives without Jill being there?"

Then create an eye-catching memo about the meeting for distribution to the attendees.

Rule 4: Allow People Time to Prepare for Brainstorming Sessions

Inexperienced meeting leaders often ask for ideas from attendees without having given them adequate time to prepare. If they are in the least bit shy, their typical responses will be blank stares, precious few ideas—and a diminishing image of you as a leader. As in all forms of public speaking, preparation makes the difference when calling upon people for their ideas or comments.

If your objective is to solicit input from each attendee, then tell them about the meeting at least a week ahead of time. Make sure each person knows what to expect and that you want him or her to speak. This sets clear expectations and gives the attendees enough preparation time to think about what they want to say. You'll get the desired results when you allow them to formulate their comments before presenting them to even a small group in an informal setting. Short, zippy memos describing all the pertinent details can save loads of time, set the tone for the meeting, and encourage shy attendees to participate more.

To: Bob, Jill, Kris, Sid, Ted, Yvonne, and Wes
From: Jean, Promotions Manager

BRAINSTORMING MEETING!!

"I want ... I need ... I must have your ideas!"

Monday, 10 A.M. - 10:45 A.M., Room 17

Once again our company is sponsoring this summer's "Diving for Dollars" charity event at the State Fair Picnic. The purpose of this meeting is to generate ten great ideas on how to:

✔ Inspire greater public participation
✔ Publicize our company's sponsorship
✔ Increase small-business contributions

• Please *write* down any ideas on a separate index card.
• All your ideas are welcome, no matter how big or small.
• Be ready to share your ideas with the group.

I'll see you Monday morning!! Muffins, juice, and coffee will be served!

Rule 5: Check the Room and Electronic Equipment Before the Meeting

Have you ever gone into a meeting to find that there were not enough chairs and you had to lean against the wall or sit on the floor for over an hour? Or have you been in a meeting where the room was so cold that your teeth chattered, or so stuffy that you nearly fell asleep? The worst-case scenario is when you thought your company's product demonstration tape was cued in the VCR and when you turned it on, attendees saw your brother-in-law's bachelor party home video. Oops! Nothing can sap your confidence and ruin your meeting faster than ignoring important logistical details that support your meeting objectives.

Be aware that the physical environment in which you hold a meeting and the audiovisual equipment you use will affect your presentation and credibility. Therefore, make sure that the room's temperature, seating, and lighting are comfortable. Depending on the time of your meeting, you may also want to provide coffee, water, and maybe some food to nibble on.

Always, always, always check audiovisual equipment before using it in a presentation. Nothing can unnerve you faster than an overhead projector with a blown bulb, an upside-down slide, a miscued videotape, or any other equipment foul-up. A last-minute equipment check can prevent an embarrassing situation that can throw your entire meeting off schedule. Yes, checking the room and audiovisual equipment and making the attendees comfortable takes extra time and preparation, but neglecting to do so can lead to disaster. On the other hand, when you know everything is right for you and your audience, your confidence as a meeting leader will grow quickly.

Rule 6: Keep Your Meeting to Less than an Hour

It's ironic that while some shy people avoid one-on-one conversations, they can drone on for what seems forever in a meeting. When it comes to time spent in meetings, less is more. In fact, some meetings might not even be necessary. Your supervisor might want you to lead a meeting for one or more of the following reasons:

- Distribute information
- Collect information
- Collect ideas
- Problem-solve in a group
- Make a group decision
- Offer recognition to staff

If you cannot accomplish the goals of the meeting in an hour or less, revise your agenda and consider other alternatives to communicate with the staff.

Rule 7: Start on Time and with a Smile

Shy meeting leaders sometimes feel reluctant to get down to business before all the attendees are present—even if that means starting ten minutes late. However, nothing can be more frustrating to busy coworkers who get to a meeting on time than being forced to wait for latecomers. Starting meetings late punishes the punctual, rewards the tardy, wastes everyone's time, and wreaks havoc on your timetable and agenda. On the other hand, when you consistently start your meetings on time, most people will arrive promptly, and you'll stay on schedule. Moreover, people will respect your authority and ability to control the meeting. If a particular individual has a history of tardiness, be assertive. Prompt his or her punctuality the day before by saying:

> *"Jean, I just want to remind you that our meeting starts tomorrow at nine A.M. sharp, and I would really appreciate it if you would be there a few minutes early. I want you to give your department's update first. Okay?"*

Don't forget to welcome everyone with a warm and friendly smile. After all, you have invited them to attend the meeting, so be a good host. To start your meeting with a little laugh, you can say something like:

> *"Good morning, folks, and thank you for arriving on time. Our staff waiter just stepped out for a moment, so please help yourself to juice, muffins, and coffee. It's nine o'clock, so let's get started because I want to finish in forty-five minutes."*

Rule 8: Control the Pace of the Meeting

Controlling the pace of the meeting is one of the leader's primary responsibilities. When you move through the agenda at a comfortable yet brisk pace, the people in the meeting will see you as confident and well organized. You do not have to be a dictator or a sourpuss to get the job done. Show your sense of humor and have a little fun, too. A quip or little joke usually makes people feel more relaxed and keeps them tuned in. When you see that an issue under discussion has the potential for setting back your timetable, don't be shy about saying:

"I can see that this issue is going to take more time to resolve than we have this morning, so I'd like to leave it for another time and move on to the next point on our agenda."

Be sure to address the outstanding issue in a timely way. Perhaps you can discuss it at a subsequent meeting, in a small group, or in a one-on-one conversation. If ignored, the person who brought up the issue will feel slighted and less inclined to contribute in future meetings.

Rule 9: End on Time and Don't Forget to Say "Thanks"

Many shy meeting leaders hesitate to bring certain open-ended discussions to an end, which can make the meeting run long. Make it your policy to end your meetings on time or earlier. If you have unfinished business, then plan it for another time or find another way to get it done. Take the last few minutes of the meeting to recap the main points covered, take any last questions, and thank everyone for their time and contributions. You can say something like:

"Well, folks, it's a few minutes before ten o'clock and our meeting is about over. Let's take a minute or two for questions and to recap what we have accomplished. I want to thank all of you for your contributions this morning. I really appreciate your time and input. Any questions?"

Rule 10: Provide Follow-Up and Feedback

Disorganized or inexperienced meeting leaders often forget promises they make to meeting attendees. To save yourself embarrassment, jot a note to yourself about any follow-up actions you agreed to. Following up promptly with any information or action that you promised builds your credibility as a meeting leader. You can also increase participation in the next meeting when you offer a few private words of feedback and recognition to those who made extra contributions to the meeting. This is a particularly effective technique for encouraging further participation from shy attendees. For example:

"Les, I want to tell you how much I appreciated your participation in this morning's meeting. You put a lot of thought into your suggestions and did a great job on your report. Thanks again. By the way, I promised you this article in the meeting."

Handling Difficult People in a Meeting

For a shy person, leading a meeting can be nerve-racking, especially if you have a few difficult people in the group. If you let them, these troublesome individuals will try to undercut your credibility by wrestling away your control of the meeting. When that happens, you'll be left looking foolish, frustrated, and diminished in the eyes of your peers and supervisors. It may not be easy, but when you prove to hard-to-handle people that you are confident and in control of the situation, they usually back off.

In many situations, you will need to interrupt difficult people. First say, "Excuse me." Then use the person's name. Always end your comment to the person with a polite "Thanks" or "I appreciate your cooperation."

The following examples identify four typical groups of difficult people that you are likely to face in a meeting, and what you can do and say in response to their problem behavior.

Monopolizers Love the Sound of Their Own Voices

Monopolizers are constant talkers who interrupt, ramble endlessly, and say the same thing three different ways. You will probably need to interrupt them to get them to stop droning on.

How to Deal with a Monopolizer

Wait for the Monopolizer to take a breath and then interrupt him or her. If you wait longer than a "beat," you'll miss your best chance to cut off the Monopolizer. Use his or her name, paraphrase the main point, and ask someone else to talk.

What to Say to a Monopolizer

> *"Paula, excuse me, but I need to interrupt you. I think everyone understands your point that the copy machine doesn't work. Now let's hear from someone else. Sarah, what would you like to say?"*

Don't argue with these sometimes aggressive and intimidating people, but don't be shy about confronting them either. Monopolizers interrupt repeatedly to test your resolve and control. Remember, when you lead a meeting, you call the shots.

Distractors Are Attention-Seeking People

Distractors frequently bring up topics or ask questions outside the scope or purpose of the meeting. If you ask for sales figures, they want to know about insurance claims. When you discuss production schedules, they ask a question or begin a story about computer training. Distractors are usually poor listeners who have difficulty keeping tuned in to one subject. They can ruin your meeting by wasting time and diffusing your focus.

How to Deal with a Distractor

Respectfully and firmly interrupt the Distractor and restate the purpose of the meeting. Then address a specific question to the Distractor to help him or her focus on the main topic of discussion. If necessary, you can approach the Distractor after the meeting and address his or her issue on a one-to-one basis.

What to Say to a Distractor

"Cal, excuse me, but I need to stop you right there. This meeting is to discuss how to keep track of the new product line. I'd like you to hold on to that question about electing new fire wardens until we have our safety meeting next week. Thanks."

Remain determined not to answer the Distractor's questions or let him or her continue talking about a subject that falls outside the scope of the meeting.

Skeptics Have a Passion for Raining on Other People's Parades

Skeptics are those pessimistic pooh-poohers who see it as their duty to find fault in everything you or anyone else says or does. They undercut your credibility, and particularly discourage shy attendees from participating. These negative individuals can destroy a meeting in which the purpose is to generate ideas and solutions.

How to Deal with a Skeptic

Don't let your shyness prevent you from stopping a Skeptic in his or her tracks. Before the meeting, have a firm but friendly talk with that person about your expectations. Explain how his or her often judgmental comments can inhibit the flow of ideas from others and that you want suggestions, not criticism. If the Skeptic's negative comments persist during the meeting, respectfully remind him or her that you are seeking possible solutions—not criticism. Then throw the ball into the Skeptic's court by asking for a contribution.

What to Say to a Skeptic

"Excuse me, Fran. Let me explain to you again how a brainstorming meeting works. We want ideas only, no criticism or evaluation. Those will come later. I'm sure you have an idea or two, and we'd love to hear them." (Pause and let the silence fill the room. The Skeptic may bring up a good point or two if pressed to contribute.)

Don't lose your cool. Tempting as it may be, do not scold, criticize, or put Skeptics down in front of the group, because they can be vindictive and may try to undermine your authority. A private word with the Skeptic during the break may get better results.

Snipers Make Snide Remarks During the Meeting

Sometimes Snipers are witty and funny, but the humor is usually at your expense. Their goal is to challenge your authority and move the attention away from you and onto them.

How to Deal with a Sniper

Do not be shy about confronting these sneaky folks, because if you want to retain control of the meeting, you will need to make them stop their undermining behavior. Call attention to Snipers by asking them to share their comments with everyone else in the meeting. Most often, Snipers will decline the invitation out of embarrassment. However, if they do share a good-natured joke, then give them a laugh and get back to the agenda. Again, a quiet word with the Sniper before the meeting or during a short break can often eliminate his or her disruptive behavior.

What to Say to a Sniper

(With a small smile) *"William, I think most of us missed what you just said. It must have been funny because I could hear laughing back there. Would you share it with the rest of the group?* (Pause. Let the silence work for you. If the Sniper declines, you can draw him or her into the discussion with a question.) *No? That's okay, but William, I need your full attention right here. By the way, I know you had a hard-to-handle rep when you had the Fulton account. How did you deal with her and still make so many sales?"*

Be strong and keep your sense of humor, but do not let them off the hook. Snipers can make some positive contributions and bring valid points into the open if you encourage them with a firm request and a smile. Keep in mind, though, that Snipers, like Skeptics, do not respond well to public criticism or chiding and can become vindictive when they get angry.

Well-Planned Meetings Are Productive and Fun

When you set your objectives, plan your agenda, and tell the attendees how they can contribute, your meetings will be enjoyable and productive. By interjecting a little humor into your meetings, you will encourage attendance and participation. Plus, for a shy person like you, leading a meeting will be more enjoyable and rewarding.

DOS AND DON'TS FOR
PRODUCTIVE MEETINGS

Do:

✔ Be informal and upbeat.
✔ Come with goodies to eat.
✔ Display finished products.
✔ Focus on achievements.
✔ Introduce and welcome new staff.
✔ Offer personal congratulations.
✔ Provide a fun theme when possible.
✔ Recognize and thank the attendees.
✔ Tell clean jokes or insightful stories.

DON'T:

✗ Argue over differences in public.
✗ Ask people to speak without warning.
✗ Be late to your own meeting.
✗ Chastise an attendee before peers.
✗ Deal with individual problems.
✗ Get organized on attendees' time.
✗ Make others wait for latecomers.
✗ Take outside telephone calls.
✗ Waste time on non-agenda items.

12

▪ Presenting an Informative Speech

"The most valuable of all talents is that of never using two words when one will do."

—THOMAS JEFFERSON

In this chapter you'll learn how to:

- **Choose a topic to speak about.**
- **Organize your ideas into a detailed outline.**
- **Capture your audience's attention with a lively opening.**
- **Use facts, examples, and stories to illustrate your points.**
- **Close your speech with a bang.**
- **Deal with nervousness and anxiety while speaking before a group.**
- **Practice your overall delivery and presentation.**
- **Avoid the ten most common mistakes when speaking off-the-cuff.**

Every Speaker's Greatest Fear

Author Thomas Heggen was scheduled to speak at a luncheon about his new book, *Mister Roberts.* As Mr. Heggen stood before the audience, he froze and was unable to utter a single word. Seeing his extreme distress and trying to help, a fellow guest leaned over and said,

"Perhaps you can tell us how you came to write your book." Mr. Heggen suddenly came alive and the words began to flow. "Well, [expletive deleted]," he said, "it was just that I was on this boat and . . ."

If you break out in a cold sweat at the thought of giving a speech, you have plenty of company. Even professional speakers with years of experience often feel anxious during the first few moments of their presentations, but they conquer their nervousness by following the two basic principles of public speaking—prepare and practice. Whether you are a seasoned speaker or shy neophyte, carefully structuring the content of what you plan to say and honing your platform skills will result in a confident and successful presentation.

Organizing Your Speech

If you are highly skilled or informed, someone may call upon you to give a speech. Perhaps a program chairperson has asked you to speak at a charity fund-raising dinner, a professional meeting, or a community organization, or you've been asked on behalf of your company to address a public forum. Whether you speak before a small or large group, structuring your informative speech with a beginning, middle, and end helps create an inspiring and memorable presentation. Speakers usually organize informative speeches into three parts—the opening, body, and closing. It may surprise you, but most professional speakers develop the body of their speech first and then write their opening and closing afterward.

Part I: Outline the Body of Your Informative Speech

What are you going to talk about? When choosing a topic, consider this advice from professional speakers: Speak about what you know and always prepare your presentation. An informative speech can be about any number of topics, depending on your areas of expertise and your audience. For example, an architect may talk about a new residential energy-saving heating device to a group of building contractors. A chef may tell about the challenges of running a gourmet kitchen. A volunteer may describe the success of a fund-raising event at a local restaurant. A physician may discuss the pros and cons of a new drug. Depending on the kind of informative speech you present, develop your topic based on what your audience needs to know.

> **PRESENTATION TIP:** To overcome presentation anxiety, remember that you were asked to give a speech because others consider you an "expert" in the field, or you are someone who can share a meaningful experience with an audience. In most cases, your audience wants to hear what you have to say. You are in a powerful position of influence because you have an opportunity to change people's lives for the better.

Organize the Body of Your Speech Around a Purpose and Central Idea

Before you begin preparing your speech, ask yourself a few questions. Why is your topic important to the audience? How are they going to benefit from what you have to tell them? What is the primary message that you want to convey? To answer these questions, learn as much as possible about your audience's goals and challenges. Once you understand the needs of your audience, you can organize the central idea. The following examples describe different purposes for informative speeches:

"I want to tell you about the benefits of our new safety program."

"I want to share with you an event that changed my life."

"We want to tell you about our proposal for an after-school program."

> **PRESENTATION TIP:** If you make a major mistake or freeze, collect your thoughts and start again. If you make a minor mistake, then just continue talking. No one will know you goofed except you.

Now you have a topic for your speech, but that's just the first step. Next, you need to organize your ideas. To help you visualize the structure of an informative speech, imagine a triangle. Within the body of your speech, the purpose and central idea are at the top. Next come the main points, followed by examples, facts, quotations, and anecdotes. Write your speech's purpose, main points, and supporting facts on a pad of paper. Now you have an outline to work with.

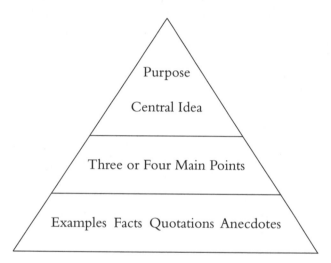

PRESENTATION TIP: The main points are the linchpins of your speech. If you lose your place while speaking, go back to the main point and then pick up from where you left off. Highlighting the main points keeps you on track and helps your audience understand the purpose and ideas in your speech.

Make Your Speech Come Alive with Colorful Examples

Now that you have a simple outline of your informative speech, make your topic come alive by including colorful examples, facts, quotations, and anecdotes. Think of a catchy title for your speech that encompasses its central idea and purpose. Continually connect the central idea of your speech to the needs and goals of the audience. Remember that each person listening wants to know "What's in it for me?"

If you are not careful, you might overwhelm your audience with too many facts or too much technical language. Use everyday words that the audience members can visualize and understand—not jargon—unless they have a working knowledge of the subject. Be sure to illustrate your main points with examples and stories your listeners can identify with. Always avoid abstract theories or anecdotes with twisted plots. Whether you plan to write and memorize your speech or speak extemporaneously, lively supporting details add sparkle to your presentation. To build the audience's interest you can preface your facts with something like:

"According to a report just published yesterday in . . ."

"I just received an E-mail this morning with some new information about . . . that I think all of you will find quite interesting."

"This fax contains the most up-to-date information available on . . ."

Imagine that you are the director of your town's horticultural society. You are giving a speech to a neighborhood group about the benefits of planting trees. You might follow this simple outline.

Part II: Begin Your Speech with a "Hook"

"The beginning and end of a performance are the most important parts. The rest is just coasting."
—quip attributed to President Ronald Reagan

For a shy person the opening moments of a speech can be a paralyzing experience. Why do you think most professional speakers

Simple Outline for an Informative Speech

Speaker:	Director of Ourtown Horticultural Society
Audience:	Neighborhood Improvement Association
Purpose:	To inform my audience of how tree planting benefits our city.
Title:	"Trees Make a Difference!"
Central Idea	Planting trees is one way that a city dweller can improve the quality of life for everyone living in a city.
Main Points	I. The greener the city, the happier the inhabitants.
Fact	A. Studies show that cities with more trees have less crime.
Fact	B. Tourists prefer cities that have trees over those that do not.
Main Point	II. Planting trees is easy.
Example	A. How to choose the right kind of tree for the city
Example	B. Finding the right place and digging the hole
Anecdote	C. Story about how children planted trees in the city park last spring
Main Point	III. Care and feeding of city trees
Fact	A. The average city tree lasts about twelve years.
Example	B. How our club has saved over fifty trees in distress
Anecdote	C. How joining the Tree Friendship Club makes a difference

> **PRESENTATION TIP:** Overcome the fear that you will forget what to say by writing the main points of your outline on individual note cards. Then turn them over one at a time as you extemporaneously present your talk. Your outline allows you to stay carefully organized and still sound spontaneous.

write and memorize the openings of their speeches? They know that they have only a minute or two to hook their audience's interest and to establish credibility as a speaker. In addition, a good introduction quickly gets the audience on the speaker's side. If, after a few minutes, people in the audience say to themselves, "So what?" the speaker is in big trouble. That is why you need to use a strong opening statement to catch your audience's interest. The following examples are just a few of the many ways you can begin your speech.

Pose an Evocative Question

One easy way for a shy person to quickly involve the audience is to ask a thought-provoking question. This effective opening captures an audience's attention because each member will answer it automatically. Here are some examples of questions that you might ask to open an informative speech.

"In what ways are you going to change how you do business in the twenty-first century?"

"What are the five biggest challenges your organization faces in the next year?"

"Where do you, personally, want to be five years from now?"

"Who in this room had a stressful experience sometime today?"

"When was the last time you did something that really took a lot of guts?"

"Why in the world would you ever want to quit a secure job that pays well?"

> **PRESENTATION TIP:** Overcome nervousness by taking a few seconds to prepare yourself before you begin talking. Plant your feet, slightly bending your knees, and smile at your audience. Now you are ready to speak.

Quote a Relevant Source

You can quote a celebrity, industry expert, humorist, proverb, or slogan to grab the audience's attention. Be sure to choose words that will be meaningful to the audience and that you quote accurately. To capture the interest of an audience attending a speech on crime prevention, for example, you could open with mention of this familiar phrase:

> *"You've all heard the slogan 'Reach out and touch someone.' Judging from the dozens of complaints our consumers' protection office receives every week, many con artists are 'reaching out' and into people's pockets. That's why I am here today, to tell you how to avoid becoming a victim of telephone fraud."*

> **PRESENTATION TIP:** Know your quote by heart so you can look directly at the audience when you open your presentation.

Make an Absurd Offer

Playing on your audience's natural skepticism is another effective way to make them pay attention. Open with a promise that is "too good to be true" and then introduce your central idea. For example, you could say:

"In the next forty-five minutes I'm going to show you how you can quadruple your investment dollar without risking one red cent! [Pause] Yeah, right! And if you believe that, I'll sell you the Brooklyn Bridge! However, I will tell you about three wise and safe strategies for investing your money that can be profitable."

PRESENTATION TIP: Give your audience a big smile when you make a whimsical exaggeration. That way they will know your comment is tongue-in-cheek.

Share a Personal Experience

While a shy person may feel a little uncomfortable sharing a personal experience, most audiences love to hear "triumph against all odds" stories. If you have a good one, use it, but keep it concise, genuine, and connected to your speech's central point. Consider the impact of this opening story that I heard at a meeting.

"I had been married five days when my doctor told me devastating news: I had skin cancer. We'd made so many plans that it just wasn't fair that our future could be snatched away like candy from a baby. That diagnosis, I'm pleased to say, was more than ten years ago and I'm still going strong because of one very important reason: early detection. My message to you today is that without early detection, my story might not have had a happy ending."

PRESENTATION TIP: When telling a dramatic story, modulate your voice so that you're speaking softly and in a controlled manner. Do not overplay the emotional aspect of the story for the sake of effect. Just tell the story as if you were relating the events to a group of close friends.

Change an Old Saying

This grabbing opener is easy for even the most shy speaker. Hook your audience by altering a cliché or proverb in a provocative way. Be sure to tie the old saying to the central idea of your speech. For instance:

> *"What you* don't know *about insurance for your home office* can hurt you. *When a water pipe broke and flooded my basement office, I assumed that my home owner's policy covered everything that was in my house. WRONG! I learned the hard way that my home owner's policy* did not *cover the damage to my office computer, printer, or furniture. OUCH! In my talk, I want to tell you ways to insure your home office in the event of fire, flood, or theft."*

PRESENTATION TIP: By varying the tone and volume of your voice, you can accentuate specific words to get your point across.

Cite a Dramatic Fact or Trend

Opening your speech with a dramatic fact is another easy way for you to make a strong impact on your audience. However, be sure to follow up any unsettling information with ways that the audience can help change the situation. For example:

> *"This glass of water I'm holding before you may look clean, but don't be too sure. According to tests conducted this month by the United States Department of Environmental Protection, drinking this water could be hazardous to your health. I'm here to tell you that tons of toxic waste go into our city's landfill each year and threaten the safety of our water supply! That is why our organization needs your help to launch a recycling program in your neighborhood."*

PRESENTATION TIP: Use props to emphasize key points and draw attention to yourself. Make sure the props are large enough for people in the back to see.

Tell a Story

While telling a good opening story requires considerable practice and skill, it can really hook an audience's interest, imagination, and emotions. The "Start-Stop-End" storytelling technique keeps your audience on the edge of their seats. Keep your story brief and include only its most powerful details. Once you hook your audi-

---

START-STOP-END STORYTELLING TECHNIQUE

Step 1: Start the story to hook the audience.
Step 2: Stop the story at a dramatic point.
Step 3: Connect the story to your speech's purpose and central idea.
Step 4: Present the main points, facts, and examples.
Step 5: End the story at the conclusion of your speech.

---

ence, STOP the story! Immediately connect the story to your speech's purpose, central idea, and supporting details. This keeps your audience interested and wanting to know "But what happened to . . . ?" Then pick up the story from where you left off and end it at the conclusion of your speech. For example, this start of a heart-warming story by a volunteer at a pet shelter would hook an audience of animal lovers.

> *"Everyone who visited the pet shelter said Callie—short for calico—was a sweet cat, but for some reason no one wanted to adopt her. Many people stopped by her cage and said, 'She's so pretty.' However, after taking a closer look, they would always take some other pet home.*
>
> *"Then one day a man gave Callie a few extra pats on her head, but didn't walk on by like so many others had done in the past. Callie turned her drooping head and gazed at him with her sad green eyes. When the man took her out of the cage, he saw why people passed Callie by for another pet: She had*

only three legs. (Pause) *But before I reveal how this story ends, I want to tell you about a new adoption program in our city called Sponsor-a-Pet."*

PRESENTATION TIP: Be animated and use gestures to add emphasis and interest to your words.

Part III: Write and Memorize the Closing of Your Speech

If you are a shy or inexperienced speaker, you might be so anxious to finish talking that you overlook a critical part of your presentation—the closing. On the other hand, many professional speakers write the concluding words of their speech because they know that the last few words and thoughts the audience hears are usually the ones they remember most. To effectively conclude your speech, be sure to:

✔ Recap the central idea and main points.
✔ "Telegraph" that you are close to the end.
✔ End on a positive note—with a bang!

Recap the Central Idea and Main Points

Even the best listeners in your audience need to hear your central idea and a few main points summarized at the end of your speech. This not only signals that the end is near, but a summary reinforces your message. You can begin a recap by saying something like:

"Before I conclude, I'd like to remind you of my purpose in speaking to you today."

"In these last few minutes I have with you today, I want to review my three main points."

"To sum up, . . ."

"Telegraph" That You Are Close to the End

"Telegraphing" the end of your speech lets your audience know that you are almost through talking and prepares them to applaud. Or, if you have done a really great job, they may stand up and cheer! The following examples send the message that you are concluding your presentation:

"I would like to close with these words from . . ."

"In just a few moments, you will have the opportunity to sign up as a volunteer firefighter. Please promise to join me and make our community a safer place to live."

> **PRESENTATION TIP:** Build the intensity of your presentation as you near its conclusion. Choose a closing statement that leaves the audience smiling and applauding

End Your Speech on a Positive Note—with a Bang!

The end of a successful speech puts a smile on people's faces and motivates them to take action. Be sure to *complete any unfinished story* that you stopped earlier. You can also end with a dramatic statement or quotation that sums up everything you have said. Be sure to conclude on a positive note and, when it applies, ask for a commitment. For example:

"Now that you know how easy it is to join our Sponsor-a-Pet program, let me finish the story about Callie, the three-legged cat. Thanks to our program, I'm happy to say that the man who stopped at Callie's cage gave her a home. She was a perfect companion for his—if you can believe this—three-legged dog! Yes, this story has a happy ending, but for many animals at our shelter, their lives are still in doubt. You can help make sure that every one of them ends up in a happy home, just like Callie, when you support this beneficial cause. I thank you and so do all our animal friends."

> **PRESENTATION TIP:** Always smile at the audience when you finish your speech. Don't just end with the words "Thank you" or "That's it" and step away. A friendly wave of your hand is a good way to say "thank you" and "good-bye" to your audience.

Do You Want to Memorize, Read, or Speak Extemporaneously?

Some speakers prefer to memorize their speeches, while others like to read them. Still others like to talk extemporaneously from a prepared outline. The best speakers employ techniques from all three methods. They may memorize their opening and closing statements, spontaneously follow a carefully prepared outline for the rest, and stop and read a paragraph or two from a business journal at some point. No matter which style you choose, practice plays a vital role in the successful presentation of your speech.

Practice Points for Poised Presentations

Nothing builds platform skills and confidence like practice—nothing! No matter how short a speech or how well you know the subject matter, nothing excuses you from taking the time to practice your presentation. You simply will not do your best if you neglect to practice your speech out loud and often. As you practice, use these simple yet effective tips to help you present your speech with poise and confidence:

- Start practicing immediately and continue right up until the time of your presentation.
- Visualize a warm and smiling audience.
- Practice your opening sentence—word for word—at least five times in a row.
- Practice your presentation aloud at least five times before you present it in public.

- Repeat the words slowly so you can clearly hear all the syllables.
- Open and close your mouth and puff up your cheeks to relax your jaws and mouth.
- Practice before a mirror, a tape recorder, a video camera, or a supportive audience.
- Use hand gestures to emphasize main points.
- Vary the volume, tone, and pace of your voice to express feelings and energy.
- Memorize and practice the sequence of your main ideas.
- Memorize and practice the transitions from main idea to main idea.
- Keep to your allotted time to speak.

Public Speaking Skills Will Boost Your Confidence

It can be more than a little nerve-racking for a shy person like you to make a speech, yet the payoffs can be tremendous for the audience—and for your self-confidence. When you organize your main ideas and support them with plenty of interesting facts, examples, and stories, you will keep your listeners hanging on your every word. By carefully crafting your opening and closing statements, you will start your speech in such a way that will instantly capture your audience's attention and end it with a bang that will leave them applauding. Then the only thing left for you to do will be to smile, bow, and look forward to your next speaking engagement!

What NOT to Say When Speaking Off-the-Cuff

Making an off-the-cuff presentation is especially challenging for the shy person. The best impromptu speeches are short and relevant. With only a few minutes to prepare, you'll probably only have time to write down your central idea. Support it with three main points, plus a few examples. Here are ten common mistakes to avoid in an impromptu talk:

- Apologizing or making excuses for what you are about to say.
- Chiding the person who asked you to say a few words.
- Stalling for longer than forty-five seconds.
- Beginning with a story unless you have had success with it in a similar situation.
- Telling a long story.
- Providing too many facts, examples, or detailed explanations.
- Citing questionable or controversial sources.
- Detracting from your main points with obscure examples.
- Revealing proprietary information.
- Not knowing when to stop talking.

13

■ Soft-Selling Your Way to Confidence

"Conversation isn't a lost art; it's simply been made practical and turned into salesmanship."

—UNKNOWN

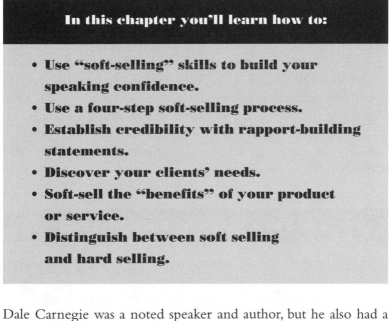

In this chapter you'll learn how to:

- **Use "soft-selling" skills to build your speaking confidence.**
- **Use a four-step soft-selling process.**
- **Establish credibility with rapport-building statements.**
- **Discover your clients' needs.**
- **Soft-sell the "benefits" of your product or service.**
- **Distinguish between soft selling and hard selling.**

Dale Carnegie was a noted speaker and author, but he also had a short, albeit highly successful, sales career. However, as a college student Carnegie was shy and, according to his mother, insecure. To overcome his shyness and reach his real potential, he joined the debate team and later got a job as a salesperson. Dale Carnegie discovered that mastering speaking and selling skills enhanced his self-confidence and helped him get over his shyness.

Opportunity Knocks for the Shy Person

Egad! Your boss just came into your cubicle and complimented you on the great job you have done behind the scenes as a children's textbook editor. That's the good news—all your hard work has been recognized. The bad news is that she wants you to "pitch" the reading program to several school district administrators at an important sales meeting. After you scrape yourself up off the floor, you explain that you are "very shy" and that you don't know the first thing about selling. "Don't worry," she chuckles. "Just give them a bit of the 'soft sell.'"

As a shy person you may find the idea of "selling" unappealing because it conjures up visions of the slippery huckster or high-pressure car dealer. In reality, most professional salespeople use "soft-selling" techniques to communicate their message and make the sale. Soft selling uses gentle persuasion instead of aggressive, high-pressure tactics to convince someone to buy your product or service. Many professionals who do not consider themselves "salespeople" use soft-selling skills. For example, an accountant soft-sells financial security by persuading investors to establish a retirement fund. For shy people who do not want to appear aggressive, soft-selling techniques are an especially effective way to deliver a low-pressure sales presentation. You can master the art of soft selling by following these four steps:

THE FOUR STEPS OF SOFT SELLING

Step 1: Establish credibility and trust with a rapport-building statement.
Step 2: Ask questions and listen to uncover a client's needs.
Step 3: Make a benefits statement.
Step 4: Close the sale by asking for the order.

Step 1: Establish Credibility and Trust with a Rapport-Building Statement

In Chapter 4, "Mastering the Art of Small Talk," you learned how to establish credibility and trust in the first few seconds of a conversation. You can use some of these very same skills when you do a sales presentation. One fast and effective way to establish rapport is to begin your presentation with a statement that shows you understand the client's needs. Here are some examples of rapport-building statements:

> To a school administrator: *"After spending ten years as a classroom teacher, I know how difficult it is to meet the needs of all the children in the classroom."*

> To a building contractor: *"I know how important it is for contractors like yourself to have building materials to a construction site on time."*

> To a senior partner at a law firm: *"I'm sure that attorneys like you value associates who can bring new clients into the firm as well as litigate cases."*

Step 2: Ask Questions and Listen to Uncover a Client's Needs

> *"Hey, buddy, you wanna buy a watch? I'll give ya this three-hundred-dollar watch for twenty bucks! Waddayasay? No? How about a nice pair of sunglasses? They're the real thing, and I'll give ya a great deal on them. No? Then how about . . ."*
> —a New York City street vendor

Most skilled sales professionals do not go into meetings and spread out their wares on the table like a flea market merchant. They know that first they must ask questions to uncover the client's needs before explaining the benefits and features of a product or service. Once you know your client's needs, you can tailor your soft-sell message accordingly.

For the shy person like you, the first few minutes of a sales meeting can be the time you are most likely to make the most common sales mistakes. Recent research shows that the following types of opening statements by a salesperson may have a negative impact on a client you are meeting for the *first* time.

- *"Nice weather we're having, isn't it?"* (pointless small talk)
- *"Our computer software is the best in the business."* (product claims)
- *"If I could show you how your company could ace the competition, would you be willing to buy our . . . ?"* (provocative question)
- *"We use Total Quality Management in the manufacture of our products."* (quality statement)
- *"Today I want to tell you about . . ."* (statement of intent)

Use the "80/20" Rule of Listening and Talking

Being shy, you are probably a good listener. At the sales meeting, you will need to put that all-important communication skill to work. Soft selling requires that you listen 80 percent of the time and talk only 20 percent of the time—which is probably just fine with you! Successful salespeople ask the right questions at the proper time and then listen carefully to their client's answers. You can ask questions such as these to uncover a client's needs:

"How many people need computer training?"

"What do you want your staff to be able to accomplish after the training?"

"What do the people who come to this facility need most in terms of service?"

"In what ways do you want to see your department increase its productivity?"

Use the 80-20 rule of listening and talking so your client does most of the talking. Remember that even if you know your client's needs, let him or her express them.

Step 3: Make a Benefits Statement

People skilled at soft selling know that buyers make a decision by connecting the perceived benefits of a product or service with its specific features. For example, a clerk in a hardware store connects a ceiling fan's quality construction (this is one of its features) to the fact that it is cooler and quieter than the competition and requires little maintenance (this is a benefit). The time and care given to the construction of the fan blades (another feature) keep them from making noise and wobbling (another benefit).

Present the product or service you wish to soft-sell in terms of how your client will benefit from its features. If you omit the benefits from a sales presentation, this question remains in the client's mind: "Okay, all those gizmos are fine and dandy, but how is this software program (equipment, training, etc.) going to help me solve my problem?"

Be specific when you link features to benefits. Begin your benefits statement with something like this: "The benefits of using this product or service are ..." Then include a few value-enhancing words and phrases such as:

- *cost-cutting performance*
- *decrease waste*
- *dependable parts and service*
- *economical to operate*
- *energy efficient*
- *environmentally safe*
- *extra features and options*
- *greater client satisfaction*
- *high quality*
- *increase profits*

- *healthier workforce*
- *fewer staff turnovers*
- *increased employee motivation*
- *lasting value*
- *maximize productivity*
- *recyclable*
- *reduce downtime*
- *reliable*
- *safe to handle*
- *save time and money*

- *simplify procedures*
- *state-of-the-art*
- *unsurpassed performance*

- *faster turnarounds*
- *happier customers*
- *greater employee commitment*

Note: Choose only three or four of the most important benefits that address your client's needs, otherwise your soft-sell presentation turns into a benefits speech that borders on a hard sell.

Step 4: Close the Sale by Asking for the Order

In Chapter 1, "Changing the Way You Talk to Yourself," you learned how positive self-talk can build your confidence. At the end of your sales presentation, you can use self-talk to help you confidently ask the client to buy your product or service. If your doubting inner voice says, "She's not convinced" or "I know he'll say no if I ask," your confidence will fall, along with your chances of making the sale. Don't allow negative self-talk to jeopardize your soft-sell presentation. Instead, say to yourself, "My product or service is an effective solution for this client's problem."

Asking for a decision to buy is called "closing the sale." As a shy person, you may find that closing a sale is particularly scary. As a result, you hesitate to ask for the order because you do not want to appear pushy and aggressive, or to hear the word "No." So replace any negative self-talk with positive messages and get ready to try a "test" closing.

Now Is the Time for a "Test" Closing

See if your client is receptive to your soft sell by trying a test closing. Make sure you have linked the features and benefits of your product or service to your client's needs. Now test to see if the client is ready to make a commitment by saying something like:

> *"Do you think the program I've described for you will help your business achieve its goals?"*

> *"Do you feel comfortable with the outline (proposal, workshop, textbooks, etc.) I've suggested?"*

"If I complete the plan as discussed, would that satisfy your re-quirements?"

Take the Risk and Ask for the Sale

If you get a positive response to a test closing, then take the pre-sentation to the next step and ask for the sale. It takes some courage, but what a confidence-booster when the prospect says "Yes!" The following examples show how to ask for the sale:

"When would you like to begin?"

"Shall I get out my calendar and schedule the installation?"

"When would you like me to deliver the system?"

Dealing with Objections

Do not be surprised if your client hesitates when you try a test closing or ask for the sale. Pausing is natural for people as they con-sider making any financial commitment. Give them time to think and DO NOT PRESSURE them to decide. As you learned earlier in the chapters "Mastering the Art of Small Talk" and "Presenting an Informative Speech," preparation leads to effective presentations. It also leads to confident closings in which you are ready with the right answers. If your client has objections, repeat the key (not neg-ative) words in the objection and then address them. Be sure to em-phasize the benefits of your product or service to the client. For example:

If the client says, *"I'd love to say yes, but I don't have that kind of money to spend."*

You can say, *"I'm glad you'd love to say yes. What budget do you have to work with?"*

If the client says, *"I can get it cheaper from your competitor."*

You can say, *"It may appear to be less expensive in the short run, but you can't get a better service policy than ours. When you add in the cost of their service policy, you'll see that in less than two years, you'll save money with our company."*

If the client says, *"As far as I can see, our company can't afford the luxury of a new system. Sorry."*

You can say, *"It's true that this is an advanced system, but it will pay off quickly by increasing production and reducing waste. Let me show you how one of my other clients bought a similar setup and increased their production enough to pay off their investment in about twelve months."*

Save Small Talk for the End of the Meeting

While some clients avoid small talk entirely, others enjoy brief and informal chats with the people they do business with. A minute or so of friendly conversation after you have discussed business usually helps build the professional and personal relationship, especially after the first meeting. The following examples can elicit a short conversation with a client:

"Bob James, a mutual friend of ours, asked me to say hello."

"Your name came up in a meeting yesterday. I heard you'll be speaking at the annual Professional Engineers' Association meeting next month."

"I understand you just returned from a holiday abroad. Where did you travel?"

"How's your golf game (home addition, etc.) coming along?"

Remember that for busy people, spending more than a few minutes making small talk at the end of a business meeting might be considered unprofessional. However, if you discover a common interest with a client, you might suggest meeting for an informal lunch (drink, game of golf, tennis, etc.) to continue the conversation and get to know each other better.

Soft Selling Is a Great Confidence-Builder

You will be pleasantly surprised to find that a reserved person like you can become more outgoing when you soft-sell a valued product or service. By establishing rapport and using the four-step soft-selling process, you'll learn a valuable new set of communication skills that will enhance your career opportunities. Even more important, you'll discover that your confidence and self-esteem will grow, too, because what you are really soft-selling is you!

HARD SELL VERSUS SOFT SELL	
DON'T HARD-SELL	**DO SOFT-SELL**
"You'll be making a big mistake if you don't buy this."	*"Please consider how buying this product can increase your profits."*
"If you don't commit to this your competitors will eat you alive."	*"This state-of-the-art computer will boost your credibility in the industry."*
"I'd hate to be in your shoes if you let this deal get away."	*"What else do your need to know before you can make a decision?"*
"Do we have a deal? I have another client who wants the machines if you don't. I need to know right now!"	*"I appreciate that this is a big decision. Why don't you take another day to think about it."*
"This is your last chance to get in on the ground floor. Are you in?"	*"Think about the risk versus the payoff. Call me tomorrow with your decision."*

14
■ Negotiating Winning Agreements

"Make your bargain before beginning to plough."

—PROVERB

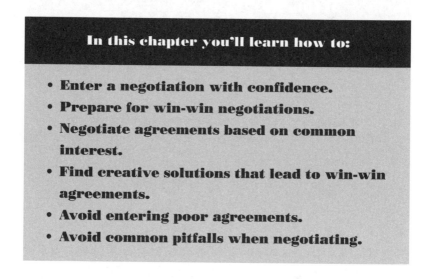

In this chapter you'll learn how to:

- **Enter a negotiation with confidence.**
- **Prepare for win-win negotiations.**
- **Negotiate agreements based on common interest.**
- **Find creative solutions that lead to win-win agreements.**
- **Avoid entering poor agreements.**
- **Avoid common pitfalls when negotiating.**

Samuel Goldwyn, the tyrannical film producer, was well-known in Hollywood circles as a hard man to do business with. During one contract negotiation, a shy actor asked for fifteen hundred dollars a week to which Goldwyn replied, "You're not asking fifteen hundred a week, you're asking twelve, and I'm giving you a thousand."

You Are Always Negotiating

A coworker wants to trade her vacation days with yours so she can attend her high-school reunion. Your manager wants you to handle customers' complaints along with your other responsibilities. You want to work part time at home so you can spend more time with your children. A big client presses you to cut the price of an order because of her department's budget crunch. Another day, another negotiation, and if you are shy and not careful, you could end up with a raw deal. Your goal in these situations is to negotiate satisfactory agreements for both you and your coworkers, bosses, clients, and family. When that happens, you have negotiated a "win-win" agreement.

Preparing for Negotiations Increases Your Confidence

Because shy people often avoid confrontations or fear offending others, they can be in danger of getting less than they want. How can you avoid feeling uncomfortable when you need to negotiate an agreement? What can you do to stop saying the wrong thing, settling for less than you deserve, or getting talked into an unprofitable agreement? How can you negotiate an agreement whereby both you and the other party are pleased with the outcome?

As a shy person entering a negotiation with a highly aggressive or skilled opponent, you might feel like David fighting Goliath. However, in Chapter 2, "Turning Your Shyness into an Assest," you learned how to identify many of your abilities and achievements to boost your self-confidence. You can use the same strategy to project a confident image and firm stance as you enter the negotiating arena. You can also decrease your anxiety and increase your chances of a successful negotiation by using the following five negotiating strategies.

Five Strategies That Lead to "Win-Win" Agreements

The key to completing a successful negotiation rests on these five primary factors:

1. Negotiate both parties' main interests—not their fixed positions.
2. Ask questions to explore mutually beneficial options.

3. Develop an alternative, or "walk-away," plan to an unsatisfactory offer.
4. Cite examples that show the agreement is fair.
5. Develop an implementation plan.

Strategy 1: Negotiate Both Parties' Main Interests—Not Their Fixed Positions

Shy or unskilled negotiators often bargain from inflexible, or "fixed," positions instead of discussing their main interests. Here is one example of bargaining from a fixed position:

> Bob, the printer: *"I need a raise of seventy-five dollars a week or I may have to quit."*

> Tina, the owner of a print shop: *"I can afford only an extra twenty-five dollars a week. That's it!"*

In this negotiation Bob demands a higher raise than Tina is willing to pay. Bob and Tina have framed their negotiation around the fixed position of money, leaving only four possible outcomes, none of which completely satisfies either party's main interests.

Possible Outcome #1: Tina Wins and Bob Loses. Bob feels cheated, so he becomes less productive and considers finding a job at another print shop. While Tina wins in the short term, Bob's productivity drops. As a result, Bob takes a job with her competition. This leaves Tina with the time-consuming and expensive task of finding a suitable replacement.

Possible Outcome #2: Bob Wins and Tina Loses. Tina feels that Bob pressured her into an unprofitable agreement. She fears that without him she cannot fill several large upcoming orders. In addition, the money that she budgeted to upgrade outdated printing equipment must now go to Bob's increased salary. Tina sees Bob as an expense she cannot afford and decides to eventually replace him with a cheaper employee.

Possible Outcome #3: No Agreement. Bob and Tina dig in their heels and refuse to move from their fixed positions. Their negotiations end in a stalemate. Soon Bob is looking for a new job and Tina is looking for a new employee. This lose-lose agreement leaves both Bob and Tina in a worse position than they were before they started their negotiations.

Possible Outcome #4: Tina and Bob Compromise. After threats and tense words, Bob and Tina "split the difference" on the money issue and agree on an increase in Bob's salary. Though this agreement is based on a compromise, both Tina and Bob feel that they got less than they need, and as a result, their working relationship suffers. Bob wants to quit when he can find a job paying more money and Tina wants to hire someone who is more cost-effective. Both Bob and Tina remain stuck in their new fixed positions until their next negotiation, when they will repeat the frustrating process.

Revealing Mutual Interests Leads to Win-Win Agreements

Negotiating from fixed positions like Tina and Bob did was definitely not a winning strategy for either of them. But Tina and Bob had another negotiating alternative. They could have created a win-win agreement if they looked beyond their fixed positions and negotiated around their mutual interests. Tina and Bob must reveal to each other why they want what they want, and understand the purpose behind their respective positions. When each person steps into the other's shoes, the chances for achieving a win-win agreement increase. Let's compare Bob's and Tina's major interests and concerns.

Bob's Interests and Concerns

✔ Pay off credit card debt
✔ Move to a larger apartment
✔ Buy wedding ring for fiancée
✔ Repair fishing boat
✔ Buy power saw for side business
✔ Needs higher-paying job
✔ Wants to learn new job skills

- ✔ Wants advancement opportunities
- ✔ Wants a position with more prestige
- ✔ Does not want to look for a new job

Tina's Interests and Concerns

- ✔ Run a profitable business
- ✔ Maintain lowest overhead possible
- ✔ Upgrade printing equipment
- ✔ Expand product sales
- ✔ Spend more time with family
- ✔ Not lose customers to competition
- ✔ Find responsible shop manager
- ✔ Keep hard-working employees
- ✔ Avoid cost of hiring a new employee
- ✔ Add a room for new equipment

Negotiate from Areas of Mutual Interest

Once Tina and Bob put their interests and concerns on the negotiating table, they can see where their interests coincide. For example, perhaps Tina will consider training Bob as the shop manager. This would fulfill Tina's desire to spend more time with her family, and it would also fulfill Bob's desire for a job with more opportunity for advancement, status, and income. When they work together to explore additional options, they will find that the potential for a win-win agreement increases even more.

Clarify Your Goals

Before you start negotiating for anything, write the answers to these questions on a sheet of paper to help clarify your main interests. Encouraging the other party to do the same can make your negotiations less stressful and more productive.

"What do I really want and why?"

"What are my needs?"

"What concerns me?"

"What do I want to accomplish in the short term and in the long term?"

"Who else has a stake in these negotiations?"

Pitfalls
Avoid these common mistakes when defining your interests:

✗ Assuming your interests and those of your counterpart's conflict with each other.

✗ Not clearly identifying your main interests to the other party.

✗ Not asking your counterpart to identify his or her main interests.

✗ Assuming your concerns are the same as your counterpart's.

✗ Assuming you know the interests and concerns of your counterpart without asking.

✗ Not listening for implied interests that your counterpart fails to make clear.

Strategy 2: Ask Questions to Explore Mutually Beneficial Options

As a shy person, you can increase your confidence and bargaining position by talking about mutually beneficial options. When you and your counterpart identify areas of common concern, then you can find several possible satisfactory solutions. Once Tina and Bob identify and discuss their interests, they can explore options by answering a series of questions.

"Where do our interests and concerns overlap?"

Mutual Interests: Bob wants a stable job and Tina wants reliable workers. Bob wants a job with future opportunities and Tina wants to hire a shop manager.

Option: Tina agrees to promote Bob to manager and increase his salary if he is willing to take on more hours.

"What can we do for each other that requires little investment of our respective time and money?"

Mutual Interests: Expand sales and job opportunities to make more money.

Option: Bob sold printing services and trained new employees in his last job. If Tina promotes him to shop manager, he can do the same for her. Tina can teach Bob how to use the store computer to track orders and let him use the company car to make sales calls.

"How can we use our different skills and resources to fulfill our interests?"

Mutual Interests: Both Tina and Bob want flexible working hours.

Option: Tina prefers to begin work before 7:30 A.M. and leave by 4:00 P.M. so she can be home for dinner with her family. Bob is willing to work later and close the shop at 6:00 P.M. in return for coming in around 9:30 A.M.

"What skills and resources do we share that can help us achieve our respective goals?"

Mutual Interests: Tina and Bob know different aspects of the printing business. To increase their productivity and income, each needs to learn more about what the other knows.

Option: Tina and Bob can team up on certain sales calls. As they share their individual expertise in answering business and technical questions, they can each add to the business's productivity.

"What creative options can we explore that will expand the total benefits to both of us?"

Mutual Interests: Bob has a side business as a carpenter and Tina wants to build additional space for a new bookbinding machine.

Option: Tina could hire Bob to build an addition to the print shop so it could hold a bookbinding machine. By expanding into the bookbinding market, Bob and Tina increase the opportunities to fulfill their interests.

Strategy 3: Develop an Alternative, or "Walk-Away," Plan to an Unsatisfactory Offer

A shy person may feel like "giving in" and accepting a bad deal if the negotiations seem to be going downhill—and, of course, that is exactly what the other side is betting on. Have you thought about what your options are in the event that you do not negotiate an acceptable agreement with your counterpart? If you identify a course of action in which you will "walk away" from the negotiations, it helps protect you from entering into an agreement you will later regret. It also builds confidence because it clearly identifies the situation in which your option *not* to negotiate is the best course of action to follow. For example, if Bob had a firm job offer from another printer, he could exercise this option as a "walk-away" plan. Bob's new job offer may not be ideal, but if it is better than an unsatisfactory raise from Tina, then it may be considered an acceptable "walk-away" plan.

Pitfalls
Avoid these common mistakes when exploring a "walk-away" plan:

✗ Threatening to leave the negotiation without a clearly defined "walk-away" plan.
✗ Developing an unrealistic "walk-away" plan.
✗ Ending negotiations before discussing all the issues.

Strategy 4: Cite Examples That Show the Agreement Is Fair

Shy people are typically more concerned about being fair and maintaining a good relationship than are their more aggressive counterparts, who want everything they can get out of a negotiation. How do you know if an agreement that you or your counterpart proposes is fair? Win-win agreements require that no one feel cheated after entering into an agreement. To build your confidence about the fairness of an agreement, find out what others have negotiated under similar circumstances. Make a few telephone calls to friends, colleagues, or other informed sources to ask for advice from someone with experience. Be sure to look for precedents that support the positions of both parties.

For example, perhaps a travel agent protests that the price you quoted her for a block of hotels rooms is too expensive for her clients. Being shy and not wanting to offend a client, you might cave in and drop your price. However, you can remain firm and still calm her fear of entering into a poor agreement by confidently referring to industry standards, citing specific examples, and recalling past agreements with the same or similar clients. You might say something like:

> *"The prices I've quoted you for the block of rooms are in line with what other hotels charge. In fact, if you call our nearest competitor, you'll find that they will charge you about ten percent more for similar rooms. You may not be aware, but your client's parent company booked accommodations in our hotel last year, and were very pleased with the quality of our rooms, the service, and the price. In fact, we received a very positive letter from the CEO."*

Use these additional sources to support your negotiations:

- Annual reports
- Association guidelines
- Competitive shopping
- Independent tests and surveys
- Industry publications
- Media reviews
- Newspaper articles
- People in similar jobs
- Previous agreements
- Price guides
- Professional regulations
- Recent comparable sales

Help Your Counterpart Sell Your Agreement to Other Interested Parties

Shy people aren't the only ones who may be uncomfortable negotiating agreements. In today's world of team decision making, your counterpart is probably not the only person who has to agree to the terms of your proposal. Typically, your counterpart may need to clear your agreement with his or her superiors, board of directors, attorneys, or others who have a stake in the negotiations. By including similar contracts or written examples that show your requests are fair, you can help your counterpart justify the agreement to the other involved parties.

Pitfalls

Avoid these common mistakes when citing examples to show a fair agreement:

Do not:

✗ Refer to outdated information or regulations.
✗ Offer precedents from distinctly different industries.
✗ Reveal privileged or confidential information.
✗ Assume that your counterpart shares your standards of fairness.

Strategy 5: Develop an Implementation Plan

"Promises may make friends, but 'tis performances that keep them."
—proverb

If you are a bit shy, you may feel uncomfortable asking your counterpart to "sign on the dotted line." The truth is, however, a negotiated agreement is only as good as its commitment to action. Therefore, to make sure that your win–win agreement becomes a reality, also negotiate an implementation plan that includes a timetable and clear description of what constitutes a completed agreement.

Following Up on Commitments Completes Win-Win Agreements

Here is where a shy person can really show that he or she is confident and competent. After you agree to certain commitments, then negotiate how to execute the agreement. During this part of your negotiations get answers to questions such as:

"How are we going to carry out our agreement?"

"Who is responsible for carrying out what aspects of the agreement?"

"What obstacles may prevent our agreement from being completed?"

"How are we going to deal with unforeseen obstacles?"

"Is our agreement contingent on the fulfilling of an agreement with others?"

"When can we expect to complete the agreement?"

"What constitutes a completed agreement?"

"What happens if either party fails to fulfill its part of the agreement?"

Get Your Business Agreements in Writing

Congratulations! You might be shy, but you and your counterpart have negotiated a terrific deal. However, you still need to complete one more vital component before you can pop the bottle of bubbly, clink glasses, and say, "We've got a deal!" **Ask to get the agreement in writing.** Most businesses use signed contracts or letters of agreement to complete their agreements, and for good reason. As time passes, people often forget what terms and responsibilities they agreed to. Furthermore, signed agreements set precedents for future negotiations. And finally, if differences of opinion arise between parties, a signed agreement can help clarify misunderstandings and resolve disputes. In the example with Bob and Tina, a simple letter stating Bob's new job description and salary may be enough to clarify their agreement to avoid any misunderstandings later.

Pitfalls

Avoid these common mistakes when following up on commitments:

✗ Relying on verbal agreements or your memory.
✗ Not keeping to the spirit of the agreement.
✗ Assuming agreements with friends or family do not need to be in writing.
✗ Not reading the agreements that you have signed.
✗ Not confronting major infractions of your agreement.

Remain Firm Yet Flexible When You Negotiate

There may be situations when emotions escalate and a conflict of interest arises between you and your counterpart. Remember in Chapter 7, "Talking Your Way Out of Toxic Conversations," you learned not to overreact or argue if you are verbally attacked, but instead to listen for and seek common ground. The trick during your negotiations is to remain firm yet flexible. If the other person tries to intimidate or pressure you into an agreement that is not in your best interests, then call for a short break. To remain cool and calm, visualize how you want the negotiations to conclude. While you may want to let your counterpart blow off some steam, don't wait too long to confront him or her. You can calmly say, "As far as I am concerned, yelling, intimidation, and pressure tactics are not part of this negotiation." Flexibility in negotiations is vital, but not when it comes to your self-respect. In most cases, if you calmly let your counterpart know you will not tolerate intimidation or pressure tactics, he or she will back off and both of you can get back to reaching an agreement.

Negotiate with Confidence and Everyone Wins

Being shy doesn't mean that you can't get what you want. Once you have your information, negotiating strategies, and "walk-away" plan in place, you are ready to negotiate with employers, coworkers, clients, or anyone else. When you know your own main interests as well as those of your counterpart, and search for mutually beneficial options, you'll be on your way to negotiating win-win agreements.

1. Go into every negotiation with the strongest "walk-away" option possible.
2. Put yourself in the other person's shoes to understand his or her interests.
3. Focus on mutual interests, not fixed positions.
4. If you reach an impasse, take a break and come back with new options.
5. Anticipate your counterpart's objections to an agreement and formulate other options beforehand.
6. Deal with the main issues, not the personality of the negotiator.
7. If you are at an impasse, restate your position and interests in a different way.
8. Look for ways that you and your counterpart can combine skills and resources to create better options than ones you are presently negotiating for.
9. Refer to other agreements to avoid getting roped into an unsatisfactory agreement.
10. Stall high-pressure negotiators by saying, "I'll think about it and call you later."

15

■ Dealing with Difficult Clients

"It is harder to change human nature than to change rivers and mountains."

—PROVERB

In this chapter you'll learn how to:

- **Set communication ground rules with difficult clients.**
- **Disarm aggressive clients.**
- **Motivate passive clients.**
- **Prevent passive-aggressive clients from undermining your efforts.**
- **Keep difficult clients from wasting your time, resources, and patience.**

Sojourner Truth, an abolitionist who helped emancipate slaves after the American Civil War, was accustomed to dealing with aggressive people. Once while testing antidiscrimination laws, she confronted an angry streetcar operator who ordered her to "go forward where the horses were or he would put her out." Truth refused to be bullied and calmly sat down in a passenger seat. She said to the conductor, "As a citizen of the Empire State of New York, I know the law as well as you do!" Sojourner Truth rode the streetcar to the end of the line, and as she left the streetcar, she rejoiced, "Bless God! I have had a ride!"

Communicating with Aggressive, Passive, and Passive-Aggressive Clients

It is Monday morning and you have meetings scheduled with three of your most difficult clients. As a shy person, you always feel a little nervous meeting clients, but these three demanding individuals take it onto an entirely other level. One yells and screams like a drill sergeant. The second says almost nothing, so you have no idea what she thinks. And the third always insists on giving you unsolicited advice on how to run your business. Then they blame you when things go wrong! After a day with these clients, you are usually ready to quit your job and change professions.

If you are shy, you may be particularly susceptible to difficult people and may avoid confronting them whenever possible. You may dream of telling them to "go jump in the lake," but if you are like most people in business, you do not have the luxury of losing any clients—even the ones who sometimes drive you crazy! If left to their own devices, these difficult clients can waste your time and cost you money. However, by learning how to communicate with difficult clients, you can minimize their negative impact on you and your business.

There are many kinds of difficult clients, but most can be categorized as having aggressive, passive, or passive-aggressive behavior. If you focus on your clients' difficult behaviors—not their personalities—you can adopt effective communication strategies for dealing with them.

Intimidators and Pinballs Are Aggressive Clients

Aggressive clients will try to intimidate you so they can have their way. These are high-energy individuals who take many risks and attempt to "win through intimidation." They care little about the needs and feelings of others, especially shy people like you! The two main types of aggressive clients are Intimidators and Pinballs.

Intimidators Try to Dominate Others

Intimidators are aggressive clients who speak loudly, often curse, and may even use threatening physical gestures to get what they want. They storm into meetings, make sweeping accusations, and bark orders like drill sergeants. Intimidators have little time for polite conversation, but are always ready for an argument. These aggressive communicators speak impulsively, interrupt frequently, listen poorly, and have a low tolerance for details. Their attitude is "I don't care how you get it done—just do it!"

Intimidators Say Things Such As:

"If you don't do it, I'll find someone else who will. Do I make myself clear?"

"You people are so stupid. Can't you do anything right?"

"I don't care what the [expletive deleted] you think. I am telling you to . . ."

"I don't care about . . . I want results and I want them fast!"

Intimidators leave you feeling coerced, emotionally battered, fearful, and unappreciated. Their antagonistic communication style is particularly hard on shy people; these verbal bullies foster an uncomfortable or even hostile atmosphere that promotes mistakes, dissatisfaction, and frequent staff turnover.

Stand Up to Intimidators Without Arguing

While "the customer is always right" is a good rule to apply when dealing with Intimidators, if you let them browbeat you, they can make you feel like an abused dog. Since Intimidators love to fight, don't dig in your heels and argue with them. Instead, stand tall and listen carefully for issues that you can address. You can curb their dominating personality if you calmly define for them some respectful "ground rules" for when they talk with you. Usually, Intimidators will back off when you stand up for yourself. If an Intimidator attacks you with a verbal barrage, let him or her blow off some steam and then follow these five assertive steps.

Step 1: Establish Communication Ground Rules with the Intimidator

Intimidating clients know from experience that if they pressure a shy person, he or she will probably cave in. You can respectfully establish the communication ground rules by using the Intimidator's name and saying something like the following:

> *"Excuse me, Mr. . . . . I want to help you. The problem is that I can't understand you when you scream into the telephone. Would you please calmly explain the problem and what you would like me to do about it?"*

If you have an established relationship with the Intimidator, you can say:

> *"Whoa, hold on, Julia! I think we can both get a clearer idea of the solutions to these problems if you calm down a bit and speak more slowly. I want to help you, but I can't when you're yelling."*

Step 2: Actively Listen and Paraphrase the Intimidator's Comments

When an Intimidator challenges you, look him or her square in the eyes and with a controlled voice say something like:

> *"I can see why you are upset about . . .* [be specific]. *That would bother me, too."*

> *"I would be upset if that happened to me, too. Let me respond and I'm sure I can help you."*

Step 3: Disagree Without Debating

Intimidators often make unfair or inaccurate accusations just to incite an argument or intimidate shy people. When this happens, avoid the confrontation by simply disagreeing. For example, you can say:

> *"I see the situation in a different way."*

> *"I had a different experience."*

"Perhaps we are looking at a different set of figures."

"I'm looking at the issue from another perspective."

If the Intimidator keeps up the verbal barrage, keep looking him or her in the eye but say nothing. Silence can be a powerful tool in dealing with an Intimidator. Stay calm and stand your ground even though you might feel like running out of the room. Remember that these aggressive people try to manipulate shy people with rudeness and intimidation. If you react with an angry outburst or defensive comment, they will see it as a challenge and escalate the situation into an argument, which they probably will win. If, on the other hand, you do not respond to their insults, the Intimidators usually run out of steam. When the Intimidator does pause for a breath, calmly repeat in a cool voice that you want to address his or her concerns if he or she will just calm down.

Step 4: Summarize Main Points for the Intimidator

In general, Intimidators are poor listeners, so you may need to repeat the main point several times. In a calm and clear voice, say something like:

"Ms. . . . These are the four issues as I understand them."

"Getting back to what I said before, I still need the data by Tuesday morning—and I emphasize morning—if you want the report for your Friday board meeting."

"I agree that those might be problems, too, but our three main areas of disagreement are . . ."

Step 5: Seek a Negotiated Compromise with the Intimidator

Intimidators usually ask for more than they really want. In Chapter 14, "Negotiating Winning Agreements," you learned to identify mutual interests, and this skill can help you deal with Intimidators, too. Without giving in to all their demands, let them "win" by agreeing to some, but not all, of their demands. This negotiating technique works only if you limit how much you are willing to compromise. Otherwise, the Intimidator will see your compromise as the first of many, and will just keep pushing you for more concessions. You can say something like:

> "I cannot address all the issues you've mentioned at this time, but if you can . . . , then I can do this for you right now."

> "If you could choose the most important issue to resolve, what would it be?"

> "Do you have any suggestions for a compromise?"

> "This is the best I can do for you. If you can't accept that or come up with a reasonable alternative, then I'm afraid we are back to square one."

Note: Do not be surprised if the Intimidator gets worked up again as your conversation progresses. If this happens, respectfully remind him or her that you are here to solve the problem, but only if the two of you can discuss it calmly.

Pinballs Are Aggressive Clients Who Do Not Focus Their Activity

Pinballs are those high-powered, aggressive clients who bounce around with so many ideas and so much energy that they are hard to control. Their minds and mouths ricochet from one "great concept" to another, but they rarely develop their ideas to a logical conclusion. While they usually do not win through intimidation, Pinballs use their aggressive style and unbridled energy to overwhelm shy people who might be standing in their way.

Pinballs Say Things Such As:

> "I know that's what I decided yesterday, but I've changed my mind."

> "We'll figure it out as we go along."

"You're not going to believe this other incredible idea I just had."

Since Pinballs make impulsive decisions and then later change their minds, they waste your time and resources by sending you on wild-goose chases. Consequently, completing any project on time is difficult when your client is a Pinball.

Help Pinballs Focus on One Task at a Time

Pinballs equate their increased activity with a high level of achievement. However, in reality, they are often just "spinning their wheels" and wasting time. An effective communication strategy for dealing with Pinballs is to slow them down and persuade them to focus on one issue, project, or idea at a time. At first it can be a little unnerving for a shy person to restrain a Pinball client, but in the end, it usually makes the relationship more congenial and productive. These three steps can boost your confidence when you communicate with a Pinball.

Step 1: Ask for the Pinball's Specific Goals and Expectations

Pinballs are "big picture" thinkers who often avoid focusing on the "little pictures," or details, required to complete a task. To counter this tendency, cast your shyness aside and politely interrupt the Pinball's enthusiastic narrative. Ask him or her to immediately clarify problems, actions, goals, and possible solutions. For example:

> *"Excuse me, Sid, but before you explain much more, what is your goal for the project?"*

> *"Helen, before you tell me about your ten-year projections, what do you expect to accomplish by this time next year?"*

> *"Sorry to interrupt you, Fred, but I don't quite understand what you just said. What exactly do you want to happen as a result of . . . ?"*

> *"How do you see this fitting into the overall goal of our project?"*

Step 2: Ask the Pinball for a Written Plan

Pinballs love to brainstorm, but their unbridled creativity can lead a shy person who is hesitant to restrain them down a blind alley. To avoid this pitfall, first compliment their ingenuity to show them that you value "idea people." Then ask the Pinball to focus on a few, but not all, of the intermediate steps and details needed to complete the task. For example:

> *"What is the first thing that you would do to get this project off the ground?"*

> *"These are terrific ideas that you've come up with, but I'm not sure where to start. It would really help me give you what you want if you could take a few minutes to jot down the key steps and what you want to accomplish. Is that possible?"*

Note: A Pinball client may resist your request to write out his or her ideas with a comment such as "I don't have time, and besides, that's what I pay you to do." You can respond to this by saying, "I wouldn't want to miss any of your great ideas, so if I can get about ten minutes of your time, perhaps we can plan your idea out together."

Step 3: Ask the Pinball for Additional Clarification

Once a Pinball slows down long enough to think through an idea and define key steps, ask for further clarification. As a shy person, you may not always say what is on your mind, but this is another situation where speaking up is vital. Be sure to say you appreciate the Pinball's creativity, but that you want additional specific input. You can say:

> *"The written steps and goals really helped me move this idea along. I've added some additional intermediate steps and I'd like your opinion on them. What do you think?"*

> *"Thanks for setting the priorities for the project. I just have a few more quick questions I'd like to ask you before I get started."*

Note: Be ready to keep the Pinball focused on the immediate task when he or she comes up with another "absolutely fabulous" idea. They have a million of them!

Stallers Are Passive Clients

Passive clients are low-energy people who work slowly and produce little. They avoid risk-taking, decisions, and commitments. Passive clients usually speak in a low voice and have closed body language. They offer almost no input or feedback, and rarely ask questions. Passive clients express little enthusiasm for new ideas and often say, "This is the way we have always done it, so why change now?" These clients often take advantage of a shy person's inclination to avoid conflict. In other words, passive clients know that if they just keep dragging their feet, shy people will probably leave them alone.

Stallers Fear Risks, Criticism, and Commitments

These passive clients work at a snail's pace and avoid taking even the smallest risks. They never seem to have enough information to make a decision or to get a commitment for a project so you can go on to the next step. Stallers defer to the opinion of others and avoid taking personal responsibility by letting others make decisions.

Stallers Say Things Such As:

"Sure I'm in charge, but I'm not really the one who makes the final decision."

"I'm not so sure that this was a good idea after all. Perhaps we should start again."

"I'm not saying yes for sure, and I'm not saying no either, if you know what I mean."

Stallers leave you feeling frustrated by their slow rate of progress and lack of commitment. When Stallers fail to stick to a decision or flip-flop on an issue, they decrease momentum and turn enthusiasm into discouragement. Stallers can make your life miserable because they know that most shy people will not confront them.

Help Stallers Take Small Risks to Overcome Their Fears

Stallers fear commitment and making mistakes. The bigger the decision or commitment, the longer they stall, hoping to avoid the situation entirely. These four steps will help build your confidence when dealing with Stallers.

Step 1: Break a Big Decision Down into Smaller, Less Risky Decisions

Ask closed-ended "yes or no" type questions that allow the Staller to make a series of small decisions. For example, if the Staller was in charge of planning an awards luncheon, you might ask:

> *"Which color is better for the luncheon invitation, pink or green?"*

> *"Do you want to present the awards before or after lunch?"*

> *"Are we going to need to rent a hotel room for the metting, or is the office conference room large enough to hold all the guests?"*

Step 2: Praise the Staller's Decisions

Stallers need frequent praise and reinforcement about the decisions they make. Without going overboard, tell the Staller that you appreciate and support his or her decisions. You can say:

> *"I'm glad you decided to . . ."*

> *"I agree with your decision to . . ."*

Step 3: Encourage the Staller to Make the Next Decision

Stallers often need an extra push for them to continue with the decision-making process, but don't apply too much pressure or they will start stalling again. You can say:

> *"Are you feeling comfortable with what we've decided on so far?"*

> *"What other decisions do we need to make today?"*

Step 4: Apply Gentle Pressure

Sometimes Stallers give you no choice but to apply pressure for a decision, and this might make you feel a little uncomfortable if you are shy. When this happens, be sure to ask for what you want and highlight the negative consequences of postponing the decision. For example:

> "If we had unlimited time and money, I'm sure we could improve this awards program. The problem is, if you don't approve the date for the luncheon program today, we'll miss our chance to reserve the banquet room. Which day do you want me to reserve the banquet room for, Monday, Wednesday, or Friday?"

> "Rather than approving the entire proposal at this time, if you are willing to approve the wording on the invitation now, then we can make our printing deadlines."

> "The situation is, if I can't get a decision on the room rental now, then we lose our deposit."

Note: Stallers speed up when you show them that their decisions get results, but don't expect them to move too quickly even under the best circumstances.

Perfectionists and Manipulators Are Passive-Aggressive Clients

Passive-aggressive clients may be up one day and down the next day. When they get angry or frustrated, their unpredictable behavior can turn nasty. Shy people are particularly vulnerable to passive-aggressive clients, because their troublesome behavior is often subtle and difficult to anticipate. These clients are extremely hard to please.

Perfectionists Set Unattainable Standards So Nothing Gets Done

For the highly critical Perfectionists, few efforts will ever reach their nearly unattainable standards. They reject most work as a matter of course and question or admonish nearly every detail.

Perfectionists Say Things Such As:

"I have zero tolerance for failure."

"This is not good enough. I want you to do it again so it's right."

"If it is not perfect, I don't want it."

While Perfectionists are hard workers, they fear making mistakes so much that they miss deadlines and often drive others mercilessly. They set unrealistic goals, and their compulsive desire for order, detail, and logic kills enthusiasm and causes tremendous stress for those who work with them. These three steps will build your confidence when dealing with Perfectionists.

Step 1: Gain the Perfectionist's Confidence with Thorough Preparation

Understanding the Perfectionist's need for order, oversensitivity to criticism, and fear of mistakes can help you avoid confrontations with this passive-aggressive client. Make sure "all your ducks are in a row," and check every detail several times before you present work to the Perfectionist.

Step 2: Substantiate Your Work with Facts and Specific Examples

Perfectionists love to test the competency of the people who work for them, so be ready to back up your work with solid facts and figures. You can combat shyness in dealing with a Perfectionist by using the following examples to set a structured tone in your conversations. For example:

"I have followed the procedures outlined in your letter."

"The information I have for you is based on the latest data from the most reliable sources in the industry. They updated it less than an hour ago."

"I have prepared a full report that outlines every detail completely."

Step 3: Ask the Perfectionist for Feedback

The Perfectionist will probably still find something wrong with your offering. However, rest assured that he or she will appreciate your attention to detail and desire to improve. You can say:

> *"I know how high your standards are. Is there any way I could improve the report?"*

> *"What is your opinion of the presentation?"*

> *"Can you tell me what you liked about the work I did for you so I'll know what I'm doing right?"*

If you are lucky, the Perfectionist may even say that you did a good job, but don't get your hopes up!

Manipulators Attempt to Control and Exploit Others

These passive–aggressive clients mislead and stretch the facts. They often use confidential information or their job position to control the people they work with. These indirect communicators use veiled threats or implied promises to get what they want. They are secretive, unreliable, and can be vindictive when angry. Unfortunately for shy people, Manipulators know they can usually play their destructive mind games with anyone except the most assertive communicators.

Manipulators Say Things Such As:

> *"This is confidential, but the big boss just told me that . . ."*

> *"Don't tell anyone I told you this, but . . ."*

> *"I never promised you . . . If that's what you read into my comments, I can't help that."*

> *"I've got some inside information that you might find extremely beneficial."*

Manipulators foster distrust, encourage hostility, and lower general morale among coworkers. Clients with a passive–aggressive communication style blame you when things go wrong and take the credit when your efforts succeed. Dealing with the Manipulator may be difficult, but survival on the job could be at stake. These three steps will increase your confidence when dealing with Manipulators.

Step 1: Never Assume Agreement with a Manipulator

Manipulators take advantage of the gray areas in communication whenever possible. In other words, a Manipulator will always interpret a statement to his or her advantage. Be on the alert for the Manipulator's vague comments, agreements, or innuendos. Listen for phrases such as "I suppose I might be able to . . ." or "I guess I probably could . . ." When Manipulators fail to meet your expectations, they often will say, "Well, I never said that I would actually do it."

Step 2: Get It in Writing When Communicating with a Manipulator

Write a short memo recapping your discussions with a Manipulator. Get written and signed agreements for all promised work, including dates for payments. You can avoid many problems with Manipulators if you force them to pay strict attention to the "fine print." For example:

"I'm sending you a letter recapping the main points of our discussion, so we both know what we agreed to."

"I've had my lawyer prepare a letter of agreement."

Step 3: Reject Offers of Confidential Information or Special Treatment

Don't let a Manipulator tempt you with confidential information. The earlier you establish guidelines in the relationship, the less likely it is the Manipulator will try to test your ethics. You can say:

"No thanks. That would be unethical."

"That isn't the way I do business."

"I'm sorry, but I can't accept your gift."

Note: If possible, avoid altogether clients who are Manipulators. Over time, the price of doing business with them is high and the returns are low.

Shy People Can Deal with Difficult Clients

Even if you are shy, you can succeed with difficult clients when you take control of the conversation and don't let them get away with their old tricks. Setting communication ground rules and using specific strategies will give you the confidence you need to work with these hard-to-handle clients. No one said it would be easy, but when you stand up to aggressive, passive, and passive-aggressive clients, they will respect you and will be easier to work with.

DOS AND DON'TS FOR DEALING WITH DIFFICULT CLIENTS

Do:

✔ Listen for "hidden issues" when talking with difficult clients.
✔ Stay in close contact with your difficult clients.
✔ Tell your difficult clients what you want them to do and why.
✔ Gently but firmly confront your difficult clients.
✔ Focus on your difficult client's behavior, not his or her personality.

Don't:

✗ Overreact when difficult clients behave poorly.
✗ Argue with your difficult clients.
✗ Discuss more than one problem at a time with a difficult client.
✗ Let difficult clients monopolize your time.
✗ Expect quick changes in behavior from difficult clients.

16

■ Facilitating a Training Session

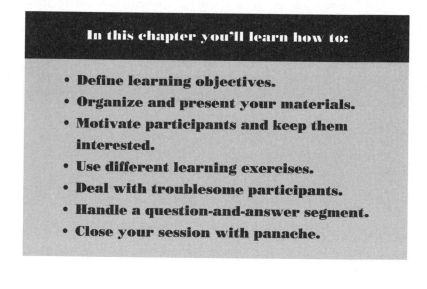

In this chapter you'll learn how to:

- **Define learning objectives.**
- **Organize and present your materials.**
- **Motivate participants and keep them interested.**
- **Use different learning exercises.**
- **Deal with troublesome participants.**
- **Handle a question-and-answer segment.**
- **Close your session with panache.**

Saint Thomas Aquinas was a famous religious philosopher in the thirteenth century, but as a young man, he made such a poor impression on his fellow university classmates that they nicknamed him "the dumb ox." However, Aquinas's teacher, Albertus Magnus, formed a different impression of the shy young man after an interview during which they discussed a variety of subjects. At the next lecture, the teacher declared to the class, "You call your brother Thomas a dumb ox; let me tell you that one day the whole world will listen to his bellowings."

A Facilitator Is Someone Who Makes Learning Easier

If your boss or client asked you to teach a sales, computer, or other kind of workshop in your particular area of expertise, would you know what to do? Even if you are shy or have never taught a day in your life, you can excel in this extremely rewarding form of public speaking. To successfully facilitate a workshop, you must break down complicated skills or concepts into easily mastered units and then motivate participants to learn.

Defining Learning Objectives

Like other forms of public speaking, facilitating a successful training session requires organization as well as a willingness to share special knowledge. Thus, shy people like you often make excellent facilitators because you are apt to carefully prepare your workshops rather than rely on your impromptu speaking skills.

To organize your training session, first define your learning objectives by asking yourself the following questions:

- ✍ Who are the people attending the workshop?
- ✍ What level of skills do the participants have?
- ✍ What new skills will participants use after they finish the training?
- ✍ What are the three to five most important skills the participants need to learn?
- ✍ What prior skills do participants need to know before learning new skills?
- ✍ How long will the training session last?
- ✍ How many participants will be in the session?
- ✍ What handouts, audiovisual aids, and props will help participants learn?
- ✍ What special circumstances or issues do you need to address in the session?
- ✍ Where will you train the group?
- ✍ Why is it important that the participants learn these skills?
- ✍ In what ways will the participants benefit personally and professionally?

✍ How will this training session increase productivity or profits of the participants' business or company?

Writing Helps You Define the Group's Learning Objectives

Writing down the main ideas that you want your group to learn will help you clarify the information you need to present. A specifically defined objective facilitates learning. For example:

Too general: *"You will learn to be a more effective salesperson."*

More specific: *"You will learn four unique methods for closing sales with indecisive clients."*

How Many Learning Objectives Should You Have Per Session?

Generally, the fewer learning objectives you include, the more time you have for example, practice, and feedback. Three or four learning objectives are sufficient for a two-hour session. Five to ten learning objectives are ample for a half-day or full-day training session.

Use the Trainer's Motto

The following formula highlights the three basic parts of a training session:

Tell them what you are going to tell them. (Introduction)
Tell them. (Body)
Tell them what you've told them. (Conclusion)

Just as you learned in Chapter 12, "Presenting an Informative Speech," the introduction to your workshop needs an attention-grabbing opening. Then you can add a brief overview of learning objectives, topics, and benefits. The body of the training session requires the most time and consists of lecture, demonstration, exercises, and practice. The conclusion includes questions and answers, a short recap of the main points, and a closing statement that motivates the participants to use their new skills in the workplace.

Part 1: Introduction

"TELL THEM WHAT YOU ARE GOING TO TELL THEM" (5–10 MINUTES)

Step 1: Use an engaging opening.
Step 2: Highlight the learning objectives.
Step 3: Identify the benefits for the participants.
Step 4: Offer a thumbnail biography of yourself.
Step 5: Clarify what you expect from the group.
Step 6: Tell about breaks and location of rest rooms.

Step 1: Use an Engaging Opening

Even if you consider yourself a little shy, you will exude confidence in front of the group you are training when your introduction is strong and smooth. Knowing what you are going to say in your introduction and practicing it several times aloud can really help control your nervousness. You don't have to memorize your opening statement word for word; simply communicate the "big ideas" to your audience. Write your ideas on note cards, if necessary.

Begin your introduction with a dramatic fact or statement or an evocative question that grabs your audience's attention and focuses it on the subject of the training session. The sooner you identify the group's learning needs and explain how they are going to benefit from the session, the more you will facilitate their learning. For example:

> "Do you know that approximately ninety-five percent of the people using computers use about five percent of their software's features? I don't know of any other equipment expenditure that gets used so ineffectively in business today. What do you think the reasons are behind this fact?"

Step 2: Highlight the Learning Objectives

Once you have the participants' attention, tell them their learning objectives. By defining objectives, you set the training session's course. You can simply say:

"The four primary objectives of this training session are . . ."

Step 3: Identify the Benefits for the Participants

Teaching people who are not motivated to learn is an uphill battle, so be sure to identify the benefits, or "W-I-I-F-M" ("What's in it for me?"), of the workshop. Tell how the information in this session will help the participants in the future. Say something like:

"The skills you can learn in this session will help you to . . ."

Step 4: Offer a Thumbnail Biography of Yourself

Standing before a group of workshop participants can be scary. However, this is no time to be shy, because you need to quickly establish your credibility. Unless someone introduces you or everyone knows you, take less than a minute to tell the group who you are and why you are leading this training session. To answer the participants' implicit question "What give this person the right to teach us?" you can begin with something like:

"My name is Jan and I am the head of production and design. I want to tell you a little about myself and why your boss asked me to facilitate today's training session."

Keep your bio short and directly connected to the training session. Include a few words about how the skills you are going to present in the workshop have helped you.

Step 5: Clarify What You Expect from the Group

Do not let any of your old shy habits prevent you from letting the participants know who is calling the shots in your workshop. Most people will happily comply with any rules or expectations that you mention in your introduction. Here is what I say:

"I like informal workshops, but I have three basic rules. First, I start and end my training sessions on time, so please come back from the breaks and lunch on time. Second, when I ask questions, I expect answers from everyone! Third, I'm not the only one in this room who has something to teach. I want all of you to share your experiences, skills, and feedback in a positive way."

You learned in Chapter 3, "Using Humor to Overcome Shyness," that laughter can make people more receptive, so smile and end your introduction with something like:

"Finally, if you want to get good marks in today's workshop, you must laugh at my jokes! Any questions? Great! Let's get started."

Step 6: Tell About Breaks and Location of Rest Rooms

For workshops that last longer than an hour, take a moment to tell the participants when you will take breaks and where the rest rooms are located. It may sound funny, but adults are particularly sensitive to these issues. An old trainer's motto goes something like this: "The adult mind can only absorb to the extent that the bladder can endure."

Note: A well-organized introduction builds your credibility, saves time, and allows the participants to see you as a confident and professional presenter.

Part 2: Body

"TELL THEM"

Step 1: Present an "icebreaker" exercise that relates to a skill or concept.
Step 2: Introduce a new skill or concept.
Step 3: Demonstrate the new skill or concept.
Step 4: Have the participants practice the new skill or concept.
Step 5: Elicit feedback, offer help, and answer questions.

Step 1: Present an "Icebreaker" Exercise That Relates to a Skill or Concept

This may come as a shock, but you—the facilitator—are probably not the only nervous person in a workshop. An "icebreaker" is a short exercise that gives the participants an opportunity to mentally "warm up" before they learn something new. Plus, if you are a little nervous, an icebreaker exercise is a good way to start the workshop in an interactive way. It is important that an icebreaker exercise ties into the learning objectives of the workshop and reinforces knowledge necessary to learn a new skill. For example, in my workshop "Dealing with Me!! and Other Difficult People" I use this icebreaker:

> *"Please introduce yourself to the other three people at your table. Then, one at a time, take thirty seconds to describe a difficult person you have dealt with recently—and no names, please! You can begin now."*

After a few minutes, I ask everyone to stop the exercise. Next I elicit feedback from all the participants about their "difficult person." This gets everyone focused on the learning objectives and shows that I expect them all to participate. I conclude the icebreaker by emphasizing the new skills they will learn that will help them deal with difficult people.

Step 2: Introduce a New Skill or Concept

Present the new skill or concept with a short and simple explanation. Use words that everyone understands and be sure not to assume too much knowledge on the part of the participants. Watch carefully for confused looks or participants looking around at one another. For example, in the assertiveness component of my workshop, I introduce and define the skill called "broken record." I say:

> *"The first assertiveness skill is the 'broken record.' This skill requires you to repeat like a broken record, as often as necessary, what you want the other person to do."*

Step 3: Demonstrate the New Skill or Concept

Now is the time to demonstrate the new skill or concept. At this point, you might feel a little uneasy standing in front of a group. One way to build your confidence is to practice the demonstration several times before the workshop. For example, I demonstrate the broken record skill by saying:

> *"I understand that you have calls to make, but I need your report by Thursday. (Pause) I'm sure you are busy, but I still need the report by Thursday. (Pause) I know computers are hard to find, but I still need your report by Thursday."*

Be sure to explain how the new skill fits into the learning objectives of the workshop. It is also the time for participants to ask any questions about the skill and its application.

Step 4: Have the Participants Practice the New Skill or Concept

Ask the participants to practice the new skill in pairs or small groups. (The other shy people in the workshop may need a little extra time and assistance to find a group.) For example, I say:

> *"Now I want everyone to find a partner. One person role-plays a manager using the broken record assertiveness skill I demonstrated. The other person takes the part of the worker trying to avoid doing the report."*

Circulate through the room to see that the participants are practicing the new skill correctly. You may see other shy people feeling a little uncomfortable during this part of your workshop. If necessary, gently guide them through the steps of the exercise until they can do it on their own. When you are helping others, you'll forget your own nervousness.

Step 5: Elicit Feedback, Offer Help, and Answer Questions

Processing exercises is a vital part of the learning process. It allows participants to offer feedback about what the exercise taught them. For example, to connect the broken record assertiveness skill to one of my workshop's learning objectives, I say:

"Now that you have completed this exercise, how do you think the broken record technique can help you deal more assertively with a difficult coworker?"

You can also evaluate the effectiveness of the exercise and see who "got it" and who didn't. You can offer additional assistance or suggestions to those who need a little extra help and address any remaining questions about the skill or exercise. Once you have completed this step, take a short stretch-break. Then introduce the next new skill or concept.

Participants Learn by Doing

Experienced facilitators know that people learn by doing and that they want practical information with immediate applications. Participants generally want challenging activities, enjoy sharing relevant experiences, and are most successful when they build on something they already know. Studies show that most learning takes place when participants practice and apply their new skills. Use the following activities and exercises to involve the participants and make your workshop "hands on."

- Group discussion
- Paired and small group activities
- Flip chart presentation
- Handouts and worksheets

- Panels
- Role playing
- Questionnaires
- Games

Handling Troublesome Participants

If you are a shy or inexperienced facilitator, your workshop can wind up on the rocks if you underestimate or ignore certain troublesome participants. The Machine Gunner, Expert, Chatterbox, or Groaner are examples of uncooperative people who can quickly disrupt your training session, undermine your credibility, and ruin the learning experience for the other attendees. As a facilitator, it is your obligation to assertively handle these difficult people. You may wish you could just ignore problem participants, but they will not go away unless you take an assertive stance.

When I first began training, I received some valuable advice from an old pro that I still use today: "Be firm in the beginning and then ease up. Never lose control, because once you do, getting it back is very difficult." This is not to say that you can't have fun. However, do not let your shyness prevent you from using the following techniques to put undermining troublemakers in their place. You'll retain your composure and professionalism if you just keep smiling and DON'T LOSE YOUR SENSE OF HUMOR!

Answering the Machine Gunner

Aggressive participants like the Machine Gunner love to challenge nearly everything you say with a rapid series of questions. They demand proof with hard data, but rarely let you finish one answer before hitting you with another volley of questions. Their strategy is to engage you in verbal combat, make you lose your cool and look like a fool. As you learned in Chapter 7, "Talking Your Way Out of Toxic Conversations," the secret is to remain calm and politely interrupt them. You can say something like:

> *"Excuse me, Richard, but you often ask more than one question at a time. First think about one question you want to ask, and I'll do my best to answer it. Until then, let's go on to the next example."*

If you don't have the data at hand, that is okay. Just say:

> *"I don't know the answer to that question, but I'll see what I can find out and let you know."*

Outsmarting the Expert

Experts want to steal the spotlight from you and take control of your training session. They love to editorialize, tell long-winded stories, and talk about their achievements to build themselves up at your expense. They want recognition, so give them a little of what they want, and promise them some attention for later. For example:

> *"Heather, sorry to interrupt you, but I think we understand your point. Thanks for your suggestions. Your comment highlights an important issue that we are going to cover in the session after lunch. Perhaps you can add something else then. Meanwhile, let's pick up where we left off. Who has the next question?"*

If the Expert says something totally off the wall, do not take offense. Keep a smile on your face, be firm, and say something like:

> *"Excuse me, Jack, but your comments are outside the scope of today's workshop. Perhaps we can talk about them after the workshop."*

Quieting the Chatterbox

A Chatterbox disrupts a session by attempting to take attention away from you and refocus it on himself or herself. Since Chatterboxes talk instead of listen, they often miss instructions and distract others. If you are shy, you might be inclined to let them continue their negative behavior, but if you do, they can end up ruining exercises and discussion activities. In addition, they can slow the progress of others. You can gently but firmly say:

> *"Fran, excuse me. I need to have your complete attention right up here. You will need to listen to the instructions so you'll know what to do next. Great. Thanks."*

Neutralizing the Groaner

Groaners stall and complain through every activity or exercise with the hope that they can avoid work. Their goal is to undermine your credibility by implying that the training session or exercise is not worth their time or trouble. If the Groaner's negative behavior persists even after you have gently asked for his or her cooperation, then give the group a short self-directed activity, walk up to the Groaner, and quietly ask him or her to step outside the room with you. In a cool, firm voice say:

"Karl, it's pretty clear to me that you don't want to be here. [Allow a short response.] *Karl, the situation is this: I need your complete cooperation in this training session and I don't feel that I am getting it. Still, I'm giving you a choice. Stay and participate without making sarcastic remarks about other people or the activities, or leave the session. The choice is yours. What's it going to be?"*

Part 3: Conclusion

"TELL THEM WHAT YOU HAVE TOLD THEM" (15–30 MINUTES)

Step 1: Prepare a question-and-answer segment.
Step 2: Summarize the main skills and concepts.
Step 3: Close with a bang.

Although you prepared and presented a well-organized training session, you still need to provide an opportunity for the participants to ask any remaining questions. In addition, summarizing the main points for the participants helps them remember the skills they have just learned. Finally, you need to give an uplifting closing that motivates the participants to continue learning after they walk out of your training session.

Step 1: Prepare a Question-and-Answer Segment

Shy or new trainers sometimes feel nervous about taking questions and so end their sessions with a cursory "Any questions?" Properly used, the question-and-answer segment can provide an excellent opportunity for you to clarify and reinforce main points. At the end of a session, elicit participation by asking an open-ended question such as:

"Who would like to ask the first question?"

"What other questions do you have about . . . ?"

"What question did you come to the workshop with that I did not answer?"

Use the following techniques to answer questions more effectively:

✔ Restate the question so everyone can hear it.
✔ Paraphrase a long question into ten words or less.
✔ Keep your answers short and to the point.
✔ Anticipate and prepare responses ahead of time for "devil's advocate" questions.
✔ If you do not know the answer, open it up to the group or to the person asking the question. You can always say that you will try to find the answer and contact him or her later.
✔ If the question is off the subject or of a personal nature, you can say, "That question falls outside the scope of our session today. I'd be happy to talk to you after our session concludes."
✔ Be ready with some questions of your own to stimulate participation.

Step 2: Summarize the Main Skills and Concepts

Repetition is a vital part of learning, especially for participants sitting in an all-day training session. Restate the main skills and concepts of your session without going into detail. If you have the time, you can rephrase them as questions and give the group an oral quiz. For example, summarizing the main skills and concepts of a computer training session might go something like this:

> *"In part one of this training session, you learned these six ways to increase your word-processing skills ... In part two, you learned these four techniques for saving files ... Finally, in part three of our session today, you learned etiquette when sending electronic mail."*

Step 3: Close with a Bang

You have about a minute remaining in your training session. The only thing you have left to do is to acknowledge the participants' fine efforts and to send them out of the room wanting to use what you have taught them. The closing capsulizes everything you have said during the session. Professional trainers often write and memorize their closing so it gets the desired response: big smiles, laughs, and a warm round of applause. The closing can consist of an inspirational quotation, some short anecdotes, or a "signature" poem such as the one I use to end my "difficult people" workshops:

> *It is to this trait of human nature to which I profess,*
> *We all can be a little difficult—me too, I confess.*
> *So by speaking and listening, your conversations will grow tall,*
> *And dealing with me—plus all those other troublesome people,*
> *Won't be quite so difficult after all!*

Don't forget to thank your audience with something like this:

> *Thank you, folks. You've been a great group and I hope you enjoyed today's workshop!*

Facilitating a Training Session Builds Communication Confidence

When you present clearly defined concepts and skills in an interactive workshop, you will motivate the participants and facilitate their learning. All your planning and careful attention to detail will pay off in a smooth and organized presentation that says you are a seasoned and confident trainer. However, it is after you end the workshop and get a big round of applause that you receive your greatest reward—the gratification you feel when a participant tells you:

> *"This is the best workshop I've ever taken."*

TEN WAYS TO FACILITATE ADULT LEARNING

1. Identify specific training needs before planning your workshop.
2. Present practical skills that fulfill previously identified needs.
3. Create active discussion as well as problem-solving and role-playing exercises.
4. Allow short opportunities for comments and questions throughout the workshop.
5. Use props and visual aids to illustrate ideas and concepts.
6. Take frequent short breaks.
7. Make a workshop agenda and stick to it.
8. Encourage participants to share their experiences and expertise as it pertains to the workshop objectives.
9. When working in groups, change group leaders frequently.
10. Put extra ideas and information on handouts or in an appendix.

17

■ Sharing Meals and Talking Big Deals

"Never eat more than you can lift."

—MISS PIGGY

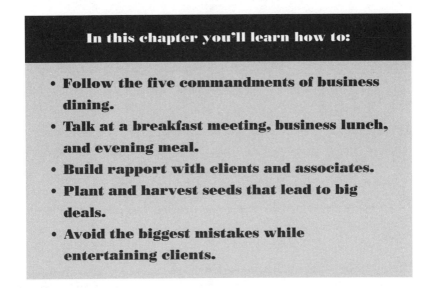

In this chapter you'll learn how to:

- **Follow the five commandments of business dining.**
- **Talk at a breakfast meeting, business lunch, and evening meal.**
- **Build rapport with clients and associates.**
- **Plant and harvest seeds that lead to big deals.**
- **Avoid the biggest mistakes while entertaining clients.**

Calvin Coolidge, the thirtieth President of the United States, was nicknamed "Silent Cal" because of his extreme shyness. While attending a dinner party, a talkative young woman tried her best to engage Coolidge in a conversation, but with little success. Finally she remarked, "You go to so many dinners. They must bore you a great deal." Maintaining his aloof demeanor, Coolidge answered, "Well, a man has to eat somewhere."

"Let's Do Lunch"

While the popular invitation to share a meal is probably one of the most commonly uttered phrases in business today, it can leave a shy person with acute indigestion. Power breakfasts, two-hour lunches, after-work drinks, or full-course dinners at swanky restaurants are popular venues for discussing deals. However, many shy people avoid these important business opportunities because they do not know what to say before, during, and after the meal. You might be surprised to find that discussing a business proposition while sharing a meal is an enjoyable and productive way to put together a big deal.

FIVE RULES OF CONVERSATION AND BUSINESS DINING

Rule 1: Know your business purpose.
Rule 2: Balance how much time you talk and listen.
Rule 3: Know when—and when not—to talk business.
Rule 4: Bridge smoothly from small talk to your business topic.
Rule 5: Consume and converse at a comfortable rate.

Rule 1: Know Your Business Purpose

Whether you are meeting for a power breakfast, lunch, after-work pretzels and beer, or a fancy dinner, remember the purpose of your meeting. Perhaps your client wants to discuss a new marketing plan. Maybe he or she needs background information for a sales presentation later in the day. Often the main purpose of dining together is simply to get to know each other better, build rapport, and network. Remember that many of the conversation tips you learned in Part One, "Kicking the Shyness Habit," and Part Two, "Speaking in Social Situations," also apply for business dining. Whatever your reasons for dining together, be sure you always keep your business purpose on the front burner.

Rule 2: Balance How Much Time You Talk and Listen

Sharing a meal allows the dining companions an opportunity to get to know each other better. If you are shy, you may find it easier to ask questions and let your companion do most of the talking. However, talking about yourself is equally important if the other person is going to get to know you. If you remain too quiet, you may appear shy and make the other person feel uncomfortable. The fastest way to build rapport while dining is for you and your companion to talk and listen at about the same rate. I use this rule of thumb: I want the other person to know as much about me as I know about him or her.

Rule 3: Know When—and When Not—to Talk Business

Opinions differ about the "right time" to discuss business issues while dining. Some people like to get right down to business and others like to warm up with a little small talk. A safe rule to follow is this: The shorter the meal time, the sooner you can discuss business. The more time you have to eat, the longer the period of small talk before getting down to business. For example, at breakfast meetings, feel free to discuss business topics with a minimum of small talk beforehand. At a lunch meeting, small talk usually takes place up to the time of ordering the meal. Finally, at a one-on-one or small group dinner meeting, most people prefer to relax for a half hour or so before discussing business.

Following the lead of your host or client is wise, unless he or she is reluctant to discuss business until your meal is almost over. If you are the "all business" type, and your client likes to chat a bit before talking business, then be ready to make some small talk about your upcoming vacation or hobby. However, you can keep small talk to a minimum by sharing some information and then asking your dining companion a "bridging question" to move the conversation closer to your business topic.

Rule 4: Bridge Smoothly from Small Talk to Your Business Topic

Tact is vital when you want to change from small talk to a business topic. A shy person like you may make the mistake of abruptly jumping to the business topic—a mistake because sudden conversational transitions can put off a dining companion. "Bridging" allows you to gracefully steer the conversation across two or even three subjects to get to your business topic. To bridge smoothly, listen for key words or phrases from your dining companion that somehow relate to your business topic. The connections between topics may be a stretch, but if possible, hook them together so you can change topics without sounding pushy or aggressive.

For example, I overheard a conversation one evening in a restaurant bar in which one person said:

> *"After I spent ten years working as a chemist in a brewery, I decided to start my own microbrewery business. So I quit my job, got a backpack, and headed for Europe to see how their small breweries operated. Ah, those were the days!"*

The other person bridged to her business topic by saying:

> *"That must have been fun research! I think it's interesting that you went to Europe to learn about brewing techniques and how they apply to new American beers. In a way, that's exactly what WorldTech does for our clients. We find and research manufacturing technologies worldwide and redesign them for American businesses."*

Rule 5: Consume and Converse at a Comfortable Rate

Few things are more irritating than sharing a meal with someone who eats too quickly or too slowly. Ideally, both diners should begin and end their meal at about the same time. As the meal progresses, gauge the other person's progress, and speed up or slow down so you reach dessert or coffee together.

You can help a fast eater relax by asking open-ended questions that encourage him or her to talk about a business topic or other subject. As the other person talks, take the opportunity to eat more of your meal. Listen carefully for opportunities to build rapport and identify his or her specific business needs and wants.

For a poky dining companion who spends more time talking than nibbling, you need to become more actively involved in the conversation. Tell a short story or interesting example to illustrate a point the other person has made. Then follow it up with a point or two of your own, and connect it to a business topic that you want to discuss. This shows that you are a good listener, have something to add to the conversation, and are ready to talk business. Meanwhile, you give your dining partner a chance to finish his or her meal. By the time the server removes the dessert plates from the table and serves coffee, your business conversation should be coming to a close.

The Breakfast Meeting

"Power breakfasts" have long been the meal of choice for busy executives who want to get a head start on their crowded daily schedule and competition. These early-bird meals can begin anytime after six A.M. and usually last about forty-five minutes. Breakfast meetings are favorites of business travelers, since hotels offer a convenient way to meet clients while on the road.

At a power breakfast, start a conversation and make small talk for a minute or two while you order your breakfast and pour your first cup of coffee. Check to see that the other person is fully awake and ready before talking business. Keep in mind that you don't have much time together, so quickly move to the business topic you want to discuss. The following example shows how to quickly bridge from small talk to the purpose of your meeting:

> "Good morning, Pat. This breakfast special looks quite good. Oh, I see you've got this morning's paper. Did you read on the front page about . . . ? I wonder how that may affect our business. (Pause for a response.) By the way, you asked me to bring the marketing plan so we could discuss it this morning. I want to show you . . . Are you ready to look it over?"

The Business Lunch

Most businesspeople enjoy going out to lunch because it offers a break from the daily routine and provides an opportunity to make contact with the outside world. Since the typical business lunch meeting lasts from an hour to an hour and a half, you have time to socialize before the waiter takes your order.

The ritual of small talk in business/social situations offers new business acquaintances the opportunity to assess each other with little risk. Small talk allows established clients to catch up on the latest industry news or chat about old times. The following examples show how to start a short and nonbusiness-related conversation at the beginning of a lunch meeting:

> *"George, before we get into lunch and your recommendations for the new computer system, your secretary told me you just returned from a scuba-diving trip in Florida. I'd love to hear a little about your trip."*

> *"Ellen, we have a lot to discuss in the next hour, but before we get started, I just wanted to ask you how your daughter's dance recital went."*

> *"Dee, I heard that you spoke at a recent conference on . . . Before our lunch comes and we get down to business, I'd love to hear a little about your presentation."*

The Dinner Meeting

Dinner meetings, whether they are one-on-one or involve a group of clients, usually include some socializing time before the food arrives. Shoptalk, industry news, and the economy are acceptable topics for most businesspeople. Other common topics of interest include sports, vacations, food, current events, family, pets, hobbies, and mutual acquaintances. Avoid discussing sex, politics, and religion. The goal of the small talk before dinner is to relax and build rapport before discussing the main business topics of the evening.

Aside from the specific business at hand, dinner conversation might also include topics of a more general business and philosophical nature. While topics about the future of his or her business go beyond small talk, many business executives enjoy expressing their visions. You build rapport when you show an interest in and align yourself with someone's "big picture" goals. If the main purpose of inviting a client to dinner is to provide an open environment that encourages musing, insightful comments, and discussion, then ask "big picture" questions. Keep in mind that this is not an interview, so don't simply pepper your dinner companion with one question after another. Base your questions on the topic at hand and what fits naturally into the discussion. The following questions can elicit thoughtful answers and encourage more in-depth conversations:

"What made you decide to go into this business?"

"Did you have a mentor?"

"How do you see your company fitting into the global economy?"

"Where do you see the real opportunities in the next century?"

"Are you working on any special pet projects right now?"

"What was the best piece of advice anyone ever gave you?"

"What was one of the toughest hurdles you had to overcome?"

"If you had to pinpoint the factors that have led to your success, what would they be?"

"Picking Other People's Brains"

Asking for advice and information is a perfectly legitimate reason to invite someone to share a meal, as long as you make that purpose clear in your invitation. For some shy people, "picking someone's brain" may sound a bit forward, but let me share this experience with you. Two entrepreneurs, one of whom describes himself as shy, invited me to dinner with the express purpose of learning all they could from me about writing, publishing, and professional speaking. For nearly two hours they asked me dozens of questions and I answered them as best I could—between bites! Ideally, the information I shared helped my dining companions move closer to their goals as speakers and authors, and in the meantime, I benefited from the meeting in two ways: I met two smart people with whom I am now doing business, and I had a delicious meal. That's a good deal for everyone! To extend an invitation in which you want to "pick the person's brain," you can say:

> "I'd like to take you to lunch (or dinner) sometime soon and ask you some questions I have about . . . Would you have time to join me for a meal, say next week?"

Closing a Business Deal

Sharing a meal during which you close a big deal is every businessperson's fantasy. The reality is that completing most business arrangements is a lengthy process. Nevertheless, the time you spend sharing a meal with a business acquaintance can lead to a business deal. Remember that in Chapter 13, "Soft-Selling Your Way to Confidence," you learned how important it is to ask for the sale. The same principle holds true if you want to succeed in this social/business situation. Once you have both agreed to pursue a business arrangement, then tell the other person you will send him or her a letter the next day restating the main points of your discussion. You can say something like:

> "Tomorrow I'll send you a letter recapping our business arrangement and where we go from here."

After you have finished talking business, don't just bolt from the table waving the signed check in your hand. Etiquette requires some additional light conversation before you end the meal. You can wrap up the meal and end the conversation on this happy note:

"I'm really excited about us doing business together. Thanks for a great evening."

Dining for Business Builds Relationships

Most people choose to do business with people they like, and what better way to spend time together than over an enjoyable meal? For a shy person like you, it may take some extra confidence-building self-talk to suggest sharing a meal with a business acquaintance, but it will be worth it. You may not achieve a monetary reward right away, but you'll be building a business relationship that—with a little luck and persistence—may lead to a big deal sometime in the future!

The Sixteen Biggest Mistakes Shy People Make While Dining with Clients

1. Waiting too long to bring up a business topic.
2. Only talking business (unless that's the client's style).
3. Revealing confidential information.
4. Arguing about controversial topics.
5. Getting nervous and talking too much or too little.
6. Overindulging in alcohol and/or food.
7. Forgetting good table manners.
8. Trying to impress clients with too many details.
9. Gossiping about the competition.
10. Using inappropriate language or humor.
11. Failing to show interest in the other person.
12. Failing to talk about a wide variety of topics.
13. Failing to listen for or suggest topics for future business discussions.
14. Failing to make smooth transitions from small talk to business topics.
15. Failing to build trust and likability through a balance of self-disclosure and listening.
16. Hard-selling their product or service.

18

■ Networking at Conventions and Meetings

"A friendship founded on business is better than a business founded on friendship."

—JOHN D. ROCKEFELLER

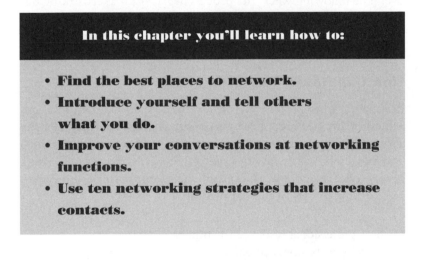

In this chapter you'll learn how to:

- **Find the best places to network.**
- **Introduce yourself and tell others what you do.**
- **Improve your conversations at networking functions.**
- **Use ten networking strategies that increase contacts.**

Lindy's restaurant in New York City was always a favorite hangout for people who wanted to network with the rich and famous. As a result, scores of reporters, agents, and tourists made Lindy's a regular stop to eat its celebrated cheesecake and to rub elbows with Broadway stars, Wall Street tycoons, and Park Avenue socialites. One evening, a gossip columnist for a local tabloid was "working the room" for a story when he sauntered up to the owner, Leo Lindy. "Who is in your restaurant tonight?" the reporter asked. "Nobody especially famous tonight," quipped Leo. "Just a lot of plain people with money."

The Goal of Networking Is to Expand Your Business Contacts

In the mid-eighties an ex-hippie-turned-entrepreneur named Jerry Rubin hosted what he described as "networking" parties. The purpose of these business get-togethers was for people in different professions and with different interests to exchange information, services, and contacts. Like hungry sharks, hundreds of job-seekers, salespeople, entrepreneurs, and other motivated folks consumed one another's business cards, telephone numbers, and names by the score. Their hope was that one or two networking contacts might lead to a job, a referral, or even a big contract. After a couple of hours of this conversational "feeding frenzy," everyone left and the party was over. The following week, the process began again. Networking became a primary strategy for people who wanted to exchange information or services with individuals, groups, or institutions.

How Can Networking Help You?

No matter what profession you are in, networking can help you achieve many of your career and business goals. You may feel shy about meeting strangers and convincing them that they want to help you find a job, make a sale, or meet a new client. However, learning how to effectively network can only help your business and career. Networking gives you the opportunity to:

- ✔ Be a professional resource for others
- ✔ Build your business contacts
- ✔ Exchange business cards
- ✔ Expand employment opportunities
- ✔ Find new clients or business
- ✔ Give and receive referrals
- ✔ Hear emerging industry trends
- ✔ Learn about professional associations
- ✔ Make friends with other professionals
- ✔ Meet industry "movers and shakers"
- ✔ Mentor others new in your profession
- ✔ Share your expertise and insights

Where Are the Best Places to Network?

Today, networking is more popular than ever and you can network anywhere and anytime. Many chambers of commerce sponsor monthly networking events. Businesses specializing in organizing networking events have cropped up in many cities. Professional associations provide numerous opportunities for members to network during meetings and conventions—in fact, most businesses expect their employees to network at meetings and conventions. The following list includes just a few of the many places where you can meet people and try out your networking skills:

- Airplanes and airports
- Association meetings and conventions
- Business and career workshops
- Community volunteer organizations
- Fund-raising events
- Health clubs
- Industry awards banquets
- Parties
- Reunions
- Social/business get-togethers
- Trade shows

Network in Informal Situations

Not all successful networkers focus their efforts in large groups. For example, I know one shy attorney who works with small-business owners. He networks at his local deli, in his apartment building's elevator, at dinner parties, while working out at the gym, or anywhere else he meets people in informal situations. He doesn't "hard-sell" or pressure anyone, but instead simply lets people know that if they have a legal question about their small businesses, they can talk to him—at no charge. If they find his advice helpful, they may retain him for a case or refer him to someone else with a small business who needs an attorney.

Four Steps to Networking

Even if you are shy, you can still meet people, start conversations, and make business contacts by using the conversation skills you learned in Chapter 4, "Mastering the Art of Small Talk," and Chapter 5, "Mixing and Mingling at Parties." Starting to network is easy if you think of the task as having four parts. First, introduce yourself and briefly tell others what you do. Second, find out about the other person's business. Third, mingle with a message, and fourth, follow up. Let's take one step at a time.

Step 1: Master the Ten-Second Introduction

Assume that people attending formal networking functions or any get-together want to meet you. The problem is, how do you introduce yourself, tell others what you do, and find out about them? The solution is to master the ten-second introduction. This is what you can do:

➟ Take the initiative. Establish eye contact, smile, and offer to shake hands. Then in a friendly voice slowly say your first and last name. If your name is unusual or familiar in some way, suggest a way to remember it. I often say, "Hi, my name is Don Gabor—like Zsa Zsa Gabor."

➟ In a few words, tell others "what you do" and "who you do it for." Avoid professional titles or technical descriptions. For example, I usually say, "I write books and give workshops for people who want to improve their interpersonal communication skills." Since I want to make myself memorable and let others know my unique approach to the subject, I often add, "I teach people how to make small talk. In fact, I'm the 'small-talk expert'!"

Here are some other examples of how to answer "What do you do?":

> *"I negotiate contracts for people who want to start a food business."* (Not just *"I'm a lawyer."*)

> *"I design offices for people who work at home."* (Not just *"I'm an interior designer."*)

"I train people how to manage stress at work." (Not just *"I'm a stress consultant."*)

"I write and edit books for children." (Not just *"I'm an editor."*)

➡ If the person asks a follow-up question based on what you have told them, briefly tell the benefits of your product or service. For example, I say, "I help salespeople increase their referral and sales through networking." Or "I teach ways to deal with difficult coworkers and clients." Or "I help shy people become more confident in social and business situations."

These other examples tell more about what you do:

"I help freelance artists get work."

"I show retailers how to make their merchandise look more distinctive."

"I help hopelessly disorganized people get organized."

> **NETWORKING TIP:** Keep your introductions conversational. Avoid a "canned" or memorized benefits statement. Just tell how you help others achieve their goals.

Step 2: Ask About the Other Person's Business
Some people you meet at networking functions may be shy, too, so be ready to ask them a few questions to get the conversation going. If the other person has not introduced him or herself, say, "And you are . . . ?" Or "What is your name?" Then ask one or two follow-up questions such as:

"So what brings you to this meeting?"

"Are you a member of this organization?"

"Are you involved in this industry, too?"

"How did you find out about this event?"

> **NETWORKING TIP:** Place your name tag on the right side of your jacket or top so people can easily read it as they shake hands with you.

Step 3: Mingle with a Message, Not a Sales Pitch

What do you say after you introduce yourself to a stranger? Most shy people fear that they cannot keep a networking session going. To solve this dilemma, prepare a list of at least five issues, trends, and topics that relate to your business before you attend the networking session. Then formulate a "message" and relate your skills or profession to these topics of conversation. For example, perhaps you own a restaurant and are networking at a hospitality association meeting. Here are some related topics and trends that you might list:

✔ Articles in trade magazines
✔ Banquets, parties, and weddings
✔ Ethnic cuisine within hotels
✔ Health and diet issues in catering
✔ Hiring a chef and staff training
✔ Hotel catering association programs
✔ On-line marketing
✔ Specialty foods for catered events

Networking Is Not Hard Selling

You learned in Chapter 13, "Soft-Selling Your Way to Confidence," that most people do not like a "hard sell." The same is true when networking. Of course you'd like to find a new client or make a sale, but your primary goal is simply to make business contacts. When you share information about industry issues with others attending the function, you'll keep the conversation going naturally and will make valuable contacts at the same time. You will also reveal more about what you do and find out more about the other person. Be sure to:

✔ Elicit information about the other person's business by asking closed and open-ended questions.
✔ Subtly blow your own horn by stressing how people benefit from your skills or service.
✔ Link your skills and services to the other person's business needs.

Use Questions Like These to Keep the Conversation Moving at a Networking Function:

"How did you get involved in the . . . business?"

"How would I know if I met a good prospect for you?"

"Who are the people here who influence your business the most?"

"What do you hope to learn at this conference?"

"If I meet a prospect for you, how can they get in touch with you?"

NETWORKING TIP: Showing interest in the people you meet while networking creates rapport and makes those people feel comfortable talking to you. Remember, most people prefer to do business with those they know, like, and trust.

Step 4: Follow Up and Make Networking Pay Off

For most shy people, suggesting a follow-up telephone call or meeting after the initial contact requires some extra effort. However, following up with contacts is one of the most important yet least exercised skills in networking. Building a lasting business relationship begins with an invitation to talk at another time. Let your fellow networker know that you want to stay in contact by saying:

"I'd like to keep in touch with you. Do you have a business card?"

"I'd like to show you a proposal that you may find interesting. Can I call you next week?"

"I recently read an article that may be of interest to you. I'd be happy to send it to you when I get back to my office."

"Would you send me some information about your services? You may have an opportunity to do some business with us."

"I'd love to find out more about your business. Can I call you?"

NETWORKING TIP: If you still feel shy about networking, think about it this way. Other people have as much or more to gain from meeting you as you have from meeting them. When you help others achieve their goals, you are networking in the truest sense of the word and, in the end, you will reap the rewards.

Networking Pays Off in More Ways than One

Although you may be shy, now you know how to network for more business contacts in social and business situations. Even if the people you meet don't become clients right away, don't be discouraged. As you continue to expand your contacts and refer potential clients to the other people you meet, your networking will pay off in many ways. Not only will it help you and your associates achieve your professional goals, but it will boost your communication skills and confidence, too.

TEN NETWORKING STRATEGIES THAT INCREASE CONTACTS AND CONFIDENCE

Networking strategies build business relationships and increase your income.

1. **Develop a networking attitude.** Actively network whenever you are in business and social situations. Don't just talk to your friends and coworkers.

2. **Move around the room.** Don't be a potted plant that remains rooted to the couch. Meet as many people as possible.

3. **Take the initiative.** Be the first to introduce yourself to others, especially to successful people who have large networks.

4. **"The sweetest sound in any language is a person's name."** Repeat the person's name as you meet, as well as during and especially at the end of the conversation.

5. **Make yourself memorable.** Master the art of the ten-second introduction. Tell people who you are and the products or services you provide.

6. **Discover people's needs.** Ask open-ended questions to uncover specific needs. If you can't fill the other person's needs, try to find the name of someone who can.

7. **Be friendly, conversational, and show interest.** People do business with and refer business to those they like and trust. The sooner you build rapport and offer to help others, the faster your networking will pay off in more referrals and sales.

8. **Be a host and facilitator.** Make others feel more comfortable and facilitate networking by introducing associates and guests. Networking is about helping others make connections.

9. **Have fun, but don't forget your manners.** Networking at parties is enjoyable and rewarding if you remember to use your common sense. One drink too many, a joke in poor taste, or a sexist remark can destroy any chances for future business.

10. **Follow up.** Keep in contact with the people you meet. Send articles and other information related to a person's interests or needs.

19

■ Networking at Thirty Thousand
Feet

"An airplane is the only place where you can't walk out on a boring conversation."

—AN UNKNOWN TRAVELER

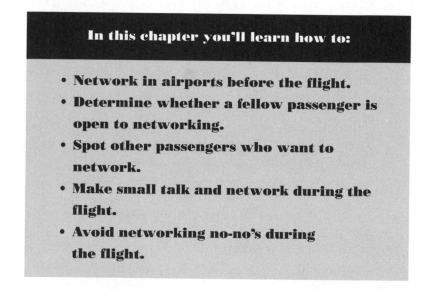

In this chapter you'll learn how to:

- **Network in airports before the flight.**
- **Determine whether a fellow passenger is open to networking.**
- **Spot other passengers who want to network.**
- **Make small talk and network during the flight.**
- **Avoid networking no-no's during the flight.**

Neil Armstrong, the astronaut and first human being to set foot on the moon, was dining with a couple who had traveled the world. Upon asking them to describe some of their many experiences, the woman responded, "But Mr. Armstrong, you've walked on the moon. We want to hear about your travels!" Armstrong replied apologetically, "But that's the only place I've ever been."

Stratospheric Strategies from the Ground Up

If you travel frequently, you probably find yourself spending endless hours in airports and on airplanes. For the shy person, these hours away from friends and family can be long and lonely. Although you may use your laptop computer or catch up on reading reports while you are away from your office, travel can be a big time waster. The good news is that even if you are shy, you can use your travel time to build your network of business contacts and referrals. Airports are great places to network because most people are waiting to go somewhere and for that reason may be willing to talk to other passengers. You can network in airports while you:

- wait in check-in lines.
- sit in the waiting area.
- have a snack in the restaurant or bar.
- browse in gift and magazine shops.

You can start a conversation with a fellow traveler by simply asking an easy-to-answer question or making a comment based on what you see or hear in your immediate surroundings. The conversational topic can center around the magazines in the gift shop, the food at the snack bar, the sports event on the lounge television, the weather, your destination, or your reasons for traveling. Be sure to keep the conversation light and agreeable—no political diatribes or complaining about the airline service. Your goal is to have a conversation with a fellow traveler and determine whether he or she is a good networking prospect. If you discover that you are on the same flight, then you might want to continue your conversation on the flight.

Finding a Networking Travel Companion on a Shuttle Flight

Since most shuttle flights have open seating, you can continue your conversation with a fellow traveler on board the airplane. If you want to sit next to someone you spoke with earlier, listen for the boarding announcement, then get in line behind that person and make small talk about the flight's departure, its arrival time, or your destination. Wait for the person to find a seat and ask if the adjoining seat is available. Usually the answer will be yes. Then say, "I'd like to hear more about . . . during the flight if you're not too busy."

Saving a Seat for a Fellow Traveler

Another seating strategy is to board the shuttle early and put a coat, briefcase, or book on the seat next to you. You may need to discourage another passenger from sitting next to you until the person you wish to talk to approaches your row. How do you politely say the seat is unavailable? Simply smile at the person and say in a friendly voice, "I'm sorry, but I'm saving this seat for a friend" or "Excuse me, but I promised I'd save my associate a seat."

When the fellow traveler you wish to talk with approaches, establish eye contact, smile, and remove the items from the seat. You can say something like "This seat is available." This approach clearly sends the signal that you are open for a conversation. If the other person is receptive, he or she will probably accept the invitation.

Two's Company, Three's a Networking Function

Taking a seat between two passengers is a good way to meet your fellow passengers. Besides, if one person isn't interested in talking during the flight, perhaps the other one will be. If you are a willing communicator, the three of you might network through the entire flight, thus increasing your chances of making a future business contact. Anyway, you'll have an entertaining flight!

Networking Etiquette on Airplanes Means Respecting Privacy

Many of the same networking skills and conversation tips you learned in earlier chapters also apply to networking on airplanes. However, there are a few critical differences. Networking etiquette on airplanes requires that you respect your fellow traveler's right not to be disturbed. Some business travelers use their flying time to plan for an upcoming meeting, or to catch up on their reading or correspondence, and do not want to be disturbed. Frequent flyers, or "road warriors," often like to relax and rest during their flights to recharge their batteries. So respect your fellow passenger's right *not* to talk with you.

Be Willing to Break the Ice

How many times have you sat next to a stranger on an airplane and felt uncomfortable? You're too shy to say anything, and the other passenger is also silent. An invisible wall of silence separates you. However, if you take the first step and say hello, you can break the silence and set the stage for networking on your flight. The person seated next to you may be too shy to start a conversation, but if approached, he or she may be happy to chat. The sooner you attempt to break the ice, the easier it is to start a conversation. Once you make the first move, you'll find out if your fellow passenger is receptive. Even if he or she is not ready to talk at the beginning of the flight, another opportunity may present itself later. For example, you can ask:

"Have you spent much time in (your place of departure)?"

"What do you like to do when you are in (your destination)?"

"This is my first time in (your destination). Would you happen to know a good way to get from the airport to downtown?"

"Are you traveling for business or pleasure?"

Working a Plane

On longer flights you can network in other places besides your assigned seat. Keep in mind that any passenger on the plane is a possible networking contact. Just because someone dresses casually doesn't mean that he or she is not a good networking prospect. To identify potential networkers, look for:

- Passengers who stand or walk in the aisles. They are tired of sitting and are looking for something to do. Talking and meeting other professionals can be a welcome diversion.

- Passengers who chat with the flight attendants or other passengers.
- Passengers who stand near the galley. They are probably available for a chat.
- Passengers who keep their window shades up. They may prefer talking to watching the movie or sleeping.
- Passengers who trade seats with someone who wants to watch the movie.
- Passengers who close their briefcase or book and look around for someone to talk to.
- Passengers who use the in-flight telephones. They may be wheelers and dealers who like to talk about their businesses.

Plane Topics

You can build rapport with fellow travelers and gain the confidence to keep the conversation going if you focus on subjects that encourage them to talk. As you learned in previous chapters, always listen for key words to direct the conversation to professional or business topics. The following topics are popular with most passengers:

Travel is a natural topic, because most frequent flyers love to share road stories.

> *"Do you ever travel to any remote areas of the country or exotic places?"*

> *"What is your favorite part of the country?"*

> *"What do you do for fun when you are in (your destination) on business?"*

> *"I noticed that you have a nifty carry-on suitcase. I'm curious, what kind is it?"*

Food topics can range from comparing elegant city restaurants to swapping recipes for home-baked cookies.

"I'm always on the lookout for good places to eat when I travel. Can you recommend any cafés with real home cooking in (your destination)?"

"If you like to cook when you're home, I know a cookbook with some fantastic recipes."

"Do you know any stores in (your destination) that sell local specialty foods?"

Hotels are a topic that allows fellow travelers to compare and contrast the places they stay while on the road.

"Do you prefer a particular hotel when you travel?"

"The last time I was in . . . on business I had quite an experience in the place I stayed."

"What kind of business services do the hotels you stay in offer?"

Hobbies reveal interests and activities outside business.

"What do you like to do when you're not working?"

"How do you keep yourself from getting bored when you travel on business?"

"Can you recommend any entertainment while I'm in (your destination)?"

"How do you stay in shape while you're on the road?"

Books, Movies, and Music are topics that help you to discover common interests.

"I notice you're reading . . . What do you think of it?"

"Did you happen to see that recent documentary on PBS about . . . ?"

"Do you ever go to concerts or plays while you're traveling on business?"

Life at Home is a topic many travelers like to talk about because it provides an opportunity to share personal information.

"I live in . . . Where do you call home?"

"I've never spent much time in . . . What's it like where you live?"

"I find it tough being away from my family for so long. As a seasoned traveler, how do you cope with being away from home so much?"

Business topics lead the conversation to networking. As you ask questions and reveal free information, listen for key words that alert you to potential business opportunities.

"What kind of business are you in?"

"What made you decide to go into your line of work?"

"I've always been interested in your industry. How can I find out more about it?"

You Never Know Who You Are Going to Meet at Thirty Thousand Feet

Until you introduce yourself and start networking, you never know if that stranger seated next to you on an airplane can help you build your business. Using "plane talk" at thirty thousand feet can help your profits soar, too, and you'll meet a lot of friendly people at the same time.

PLANE-TALK NETWORKING NO-NO'S

While networking on airplanes is a great way to make business contacts, avoid the following mistakes. DO NOT:

✗ Talk nonstop about yourself or your business.

✗ Feel compelled to talk or network for the entire flight.

✗ Get pushy about meeting socially.

✗ Pump your fellow passengers for professional advice.

✗ Bad-mouth your competition or gossip about your associates.

✗ Drink or eat excessively during the flight.

✗ Exaggerate your personal achievements or those of your company.

✗ Give your fellow passenger the "brush-off" just because he or she is not dressed in business attire.

✗ Talk about your personal problems.

■ Conclusion

Talking with Confidence Means You're Not Shy Anymore

Your communication skills are like your muscles: The more you exercise them, the more powerful they become. As you increase your ability to talk in social and business situations, your confidence will also grow stronger, and you'll feel less shy. At times you may still feel nervous on the inside, but on the outside you communicate an interested, interesting, confident, and friendly image to everyone you meet—friends, family, clients, and strangers. Each time you practice the techniques in this book, you will move one step closer to overcoming your lifelong struggle with shyness. Talking with confidence will lead you to many new social and business opportunities, but the most important reward is when you say to yourself, "I used to be shy—but not anymore!"

■ Suggested Reading

Berent, Jonathan, *Beyond Shyness: How to Conquer Social Anxiety* (Simon & Schuster, 1993).

Bramson, Robert, *Coping with Difficult People* (Bantam Doubleday Dell, 1981).

Gabor, Don, *How to Start a Conversation and Make Friends* (Simon & Schuster, 1983).

———, *How to Start a Conversation* (Random House Audio Publishing, 1988).

———, *How to Talk to the People You Love* (Simon & Schuster, 1989).

———, *Speaking Your Mind in 101 Difficult Situations* (Simon & Schuster, 1994).

Griffin, Jack, *How to Say It Best* (Prentice-Hall, 1994).

Hirsch, Arlene, *National Business Employment Weekly: Interviewing* (John Wiley & Sons, Inc., 1994).

Martin, Judith, *Miss Manners' Guide to Excruciatingly Correct Behavior* (Warner Books, 1982).

Newstrom, John, and Edward Scannell, *Games Trainers Play* (McGraw-Hill, 1980).

Pardee, Bette, *Pardee Guide to Great Entertaining* (Peachtree Publishers, 1990).

Roane, Susan, *How to Work a Room* (Warner Books, 1988).

Sarnoff, Dorothy, *Speech Can Change Your Life* (Dell, 1972).

Schwartz, Arnold, *Dynamic Professional Selling* (Plume, 1990).

Walters, Lilly, *What to Say When You're Dying on the Platform* (McGraw-Hill, 1995).

Zimbardo, Philip, *Shyness* (Jove/HBJ, 1977).

■ Index

■ About the Author

Don Gabor is an author, communications trainer, and "small talk" expert. He has been writing and speaking about the art of conversation since 1980 and presents workshops and keynote speeches to associations, businesses, corporations, and universities. He is a member of the National Speakers Association and the American Society for Training and Development, and is a frequent media guest and spokesperson.

Don Gabor is dedicated to helping people of all ages achieve personal and professional success by improving their interpersonal communication skills. He founded Conversation Arts Media in 1991 to realize this goal.

Find out how you can arrange for Don Gabor to speak to your group. You can also receive his free conversation tip sheet, "50 Ways to Improve Your Conversations," and more information about his books and tapes. Please write or call:

Don Gabor
Conversation Arts Media
P.O. Box 150-715
Brooklyn, NY 11215

718-768-0824